About The Author

Addy Kasi is the founder
Upperview Ministries Inte   ... ...pperview
Schools of Ministry Worldwide, The Leading Couples
(LeCos) and Pastors For Pastors. Bishop-General Addy
Kasi began to minister at the age of 16 when God released His anointing upon him. Led by this heavenly
anointing, young Addy Kasi travelled places preaching
the Gospel confirmed by real signs and wonders which
many people, old and young, testify of today.

To date, Bishop-General Addy Kasi has reached many
villages, townships, cities countries and continents
with the Gospel of peace. His message offers the hope
in Christ Jesus through love with the powerful vision
theme 'Called To Love'.

There are many people who believe they are still
alive today owing to God's grace released upon them
through the ministering of Bishop-General Addy Kasi.

An acknowledged humble man of God, Addy Kasi is a
husband, father and family man. He is a pastor, a men-
tor, a teacher and to many, the humble father of multi-
tudes who seek guidance and direction from him.

A holder of a Bachelor of Laws Degree (LLB), Master
of Laws Degree (LLM) as well as a Doctorate in Theol-
ogy, Addy Kasi is also an Accredited International Civil
and Commercial Mediator. At the time of writing Addy

Kasi, also a Law Tutor, was progressing with his thesis for his PhD in Law (Corporate Governance).

Bishop-General Addy Kasi offers valued support to many ministries and churches which have submitted to move under his wise spiritual guidance.

This great book, 'From The Womb With God', is Addy Kasi's powerful piece of work detailing the perception of this General of God into how God puts His mark on a person right from the mother's womb for His Kingdom purposes. I am convinced you will be blessed as you read.

Pastor Mel Gray

FROM THE WOMB
WITH GOD

FROM THE AUTHOR
OF
HELLO JONAH

From The Womb With God

by

Bishop-General
Addy Kasi

From The Womb With God

Written By
Bishop-General
Addy Kasi
bishop@upperview.org

Published & Distributed By
UpperVision Inc
books@upperview.org

United Kingdom
46-48 George St, Luton
LU1 2AZ

Africa Centre
39 Baines Ave, Harare
Zimbabwe

ISBN 978-0-9954663-0-2

Printed by Biddles Books, King's Lynn, Norfolk PE32 1SF

Edited by   Pastor Mel Gray
                        Abigal Mujakachi

Arranged by   Pastor Matt Mtanga
                        Bridget Gavanga
                        Pastor Mel Gray

A Note From The Author

Intrigued by the amazing story of the twins of Rebekah, I indeed was pushed to share with you the fundamentals of how God's involvement with the called can be traced right from the womb, even as He has declared that "before you were in your mother's womb I have known you" (Jer 1:5). I have carried in my heart the burden to share with us all that we are not ordinary but God's foreknown ones. This makes the title of this book " From The Womb With God" most appropriate.

Rebekah had always known that what was in her womb was from God, so she went back to Him who had started what was growing in her at the time she did not understand the rigorous fights taking place there. She became God's connection and representative who would understand that nations and not mere babies were inside her womb and that the younger was to prevail. The actions of Rebekah, the mother of the world's most famous twins, Esau and Jacob, would always be premised on this knowledge.

It is my conviction, also, that I should come in defence of God's Jacob, upon who we may have recklessly heaped condemnation, calling him a fraudster and a thief. We need to take note that by cursing Jacob many get themselves cursed as he can only be blessed, carrying as he does, the blessings of Abraham (Gen 12:3, 28:14).

After all, Jacob is now part of God's memorial name, to wit "the God of Abraham, the God of Isaac and the God of Jacob" (Exo 3:15, Num 23:8). Note that God has insisted being the God of Jacob even after the change of name to Israel. Contrary to popular thought, Jacob as a name never meant a thief but only refers to clutching the heel at birth (Gen 25:26).

You are born to make it. You are born now through Jesus Christ to overcome. In Jesus Christ you were born to be great so that you can now declare "I was born like this". You will find empowerment in the reading of this book and I pray every time you read, even a few lines, you meet with God's empowering grace through Jesus Christ.

His servant for your sake,

Addy Kasi

Contents

Chapter One

The Battle of the Innocent

To a barren woman, the daughter of Bethuel the Syrian, the sister of Laban, Rebekah, was born two "nations". It all started in the womb. Isaac, bothered by his wife's continued barrenness, prayed for her unto the Lord who opened her womb and she conceived. *(Gen 25:21) And Isaac prayed to Jehovah for his wife, because she was barren. And Jehovah heard him, and Rebekah his wife conceived.* The story begins from utter hopelessness. From barrenness to a double delivery! She conceived and it became apparent that she had two inside her womb.

Having two would not have been the major mystery to contend with although during those days such situations were perceived with a degree of unease. Rebekah was soon to learn that she not only had two foetuses inside her and not only two brothers, but "two nations". Two peoples! She hardly had occasion to celebrate her conception, for soon a war was to break out inside the womb. The nations struggled between themselves fiercely. It was a war whose intensity only the mother could feel. How else could she account for the desperate struggles and fights that continued unabated in her womb? Obviously, whoever she may have sought help from would only have indicated to her that hers was an unprecedented situation. No living person would ever have anticipated a war between the most innocent. How could mere foetuses fight like grownups with reason to compete or argue? It's not as if they were born yet. They had no thoughts or knowledge regarding life. They did not eat from a plate but were still connected separately to the placenta by the umbilical code for feeding, a natural process. Where in the womb would they get such strength to fiercely struggle? It creates further anxiety as to whether they already were able to communicate words to each other. What words did they exchange while they still floated on the waters of the unborn?

The woman was not carrying an ordinary pregnancy. Desperate to find a ceasefire for the raging battles which even the United Nations Security Council, if there was any such, could not have understood, she decided to inquire from the Lord who advised her not to treat her pregnancy as ordinary, but that she had inside her, "two nations", two peoples. As if that was not hard enough to comprehend, she was also advised that the elder would serve the younger. *(Gen 25:22) And the children struggled together within her; and she said, if it be so, why am I thus? And she went to enquire of the LORD. (Gen 25:23) And the LORD said unto her, two nations are in thy womb, and two manner of people shall be separated from thy bowels; and the one people shall be stronger than the other peo-*

ple; and the elder shall serve the younger. This message from God was to permanently change Rebekah's perception regarding the pregnancy. She would now know for real that her womb had become a battle ground and that one of the nations was the winner of this worrisome war. It was going to be the nation represented by the boy who would come, not first, but last in this impending twin delivery.

From this point on, it was going to be Rebekah's lonely curiosity how the utterances of God would come to pass. She would have felt so honoured for God to reveal such heavy plans to her. She knew she was going to be part of the great plan. Why would God confidentially announce to her such unusual news? Why, amidst all women, should she be the one to carry nations while others carry babies? If she had found favour to carry the nations, then she surely was to be involved in how the nations were to start off as the Lord had said they were to be separated from her bowels *(Gen 25:23)*. You can imagine with what excitement she looked at her tummy grow. She, by now, should know what time the nations fight and what time they take a temporal cease fire. When other pregnant women discussed what they expected their babies to be like when born, she would only remember the description of what her own would be from her conversations with the Lord. As the delivery days drew closer, Rebekah would have been seeking wisdom on how to handle the situation after birth. She would have spent more time in prayer to get an understanding of the delicate circumstances anticipated on the day of delivery. She went into labour and the boys, the peoples or the nations began their journey out. It is intriguing that after the first, who they called Esau, followed the second with his hand clutching the heel of the first. They named him Jacob for this reason. It was clear at birth that the two had some unfinished business.

It would appear Jacob was trying to come out first as he pulled his brother's leg or was preventing him from running away with the treasure, if at all that is the fitting description. He was fighting for the birth right over which he later prevailed. Isaac, the father of the twins, loved Esau as was the custom. The first born boy was the inheritor of the father's legacy. As an obvious heir, he was expected to be the next head of the family. Entitled to a double portion on the wealth of the father, the first born boy was supposed to understand the goings on of the family and have fair knowledge of the wars that were fought by his father in order to carry on at his death. Simply by virtue of birth right, the first boy was entitled to the throne of his father regardless of any presence of qualities or lack of them. In this case, much more was at stake than the usual. It was about the covenant. God had made a covenant with Abraham that his descendants would be as the sand on the seashore and the stars of the heavens and that they would be blessed. The descendants were to possess a promised land and be a peculiar people on earth. Abraham's seed would possess the gate of his enemy. All nations were to be blessed in Abraham's seed and this was to come from Isaac the son of promise. *(Gen 22:15) And the angel of the LORD called unto Abraham a second time out of heaven, (Gen 22:16) and said: 'By Myself have I sworn, saith the LORD, because thou hast done this thing, and hast not withheld thy son, thine only son, (Gen 22:17) that in blessing I will bless thee, and in multiplying I will multiply thy seed as the stars of the heaven, and as the sand which is upon the sea-shore; and thy seed shall possess the gate of his enemies; (Gen 22:18) and in thy seed shall all the nations of the earth be blessed; because thou hearkened to My voice.'*

Although Abraham later had other children with Keturah, he gave all he had to Isaac the son of the promise. *(Gen 25:5) Abraham gave all he had to Isaac.* God followed Isaac wherever he went and confirmed the blessing as He had sworn to Abraham. *(Gen 26:3) Sojourn in this land, and I will be with you and will bless you, for to you and your offspring I will give all these lands, and I will establish the oath that I swore to Abraham your father. (Gen 26:4) I will multiply your offspring as the stars of heaven and will give to your offspring all these lands. And in your offspring all the nations of the earth shall be blessed.* So far, the covenant has been peacefully handed over to Isaac who met no challenges whatsoever, as he was clearly the son of promise. We have learnt that Isaac loved Esau more than Jacob and Esau was a successful hunter whose game was enjoyed by his aging father while Jacob stayed in the tent and learnt to cook like his mother. The blessings of Abraham were to flow forever in the manner which God designed them. They started from Abraham and went to his seed Isaac and needed to flow by the descending order according to birth. Esau was the next in line. The Lord God would be known as the God of Abraham, the God of Isaac and the God of Esau. If any writings were being updated in anticipation of Isaac's death, they would have read like that. Even Esau himself would probably have been playing around with coming to terms with becoming a founding Patriarch and rehearsing how to be a channel of blessing as he was about to be the next one who would also hand the blessings to the next generation. The point to note is that the blessings were God's blessings to Abraham strengthened and guided by a covenant. God had sworn and Abraham had also sworn by accepting and agreeing to do the impossible that God ordered him to do. He had obeyed and agreed to move from his kindred and had believed the word of God that he would bear a child with Sarah at a biologically impossible age for her. He also had passed a crucial obedience and compliance test by heeding the Lord's call for him to offer his only son Isaac born after years of anticipation when hopes for Sarah to conceive again were further away than ever. They had hoped against hope. Covenant remained the main issue. Obedience was paramount. All these qualities would guarantee God's performance of the promises. Abraham had obeyed God and kept covenant. *(Gen 26:5) because Abraham obeyed my voice and kept my charge, my commandments, my statutes, and my laws."*

Chapter Two

The Jacob Ministry

I n the process of time, so much has been said about Jacob that the real intentions of God and His plans have been seriously distorted. It has become public gospel that Jacob was a thief. He is branded as having been dishonest. When a fellow Christian exhibits greed and violence, the interpretation is that he or she has taken after Jacob. So much goes on and message after message, speakers condemn Jacob. What is it that Jacob did wrong? Where did he fall out with the believers of today when in him they are to be blessed? He is the seed of Abraham, the offspring of Isaac. The words of the Lord to Isaac: *(Gen 26:4) And in your offspring all the nations of the earth shall be blessed. To Abraham He had said :(Gen 22:18) And in your Seed shall all the nations of the earth be blessed.*

Contrary to popular belief, there is no trace whatsoever that Jacob was a crook, a thief or a violent man. At a tender age, Jacob is described as a gentle young man who stayed in the tents while the stronger Esau went hunting. It's Esau whose countenance was ruddy and violent, which is still acceptable for a hunter who faced different predators in the bushes. Esau was the main man. Jacob was shy and kept closer to home. There was nothing wrong with that, considering Esau was the elder. *(Gen 25:27) And the boys grew: and Esau was a cunning hunter, a man of the field; and Jacob was a plain man, dwelling in tents*.

Of course Isaac's blessing of Jacob brings all these innocently inappropriate theories that Jacob was not good and was violent and dishonest. We will need to accept certain basics in this whole story before we get deluded by natural instincts. The one big thing is that Jacob was the first born son of Isaac and deserved to be blessed like so. Yes, the first born, and I will show you how very soon. Before we go to God and his designs, let's spend a little bit of time with the boys, the twins, dubbed 'nations' or 'peoples' *(Gen 25:23)*. Remember that the blessings are not coming other than by covenant. We are today children of Abraham not by natural process but by covenant. Sarah was the mother of Isaac although she was already dead in the uterus. She became his mother not by natural process but by covenant. In the same manner Isaac was offered to God but was only saved when God provided a ram which Abraham, at the command of God, looked at and found entangled by its own horns into the bushes. Therefore, it is true that Isaac was offered at the altar and by covenant God resurrected him as upon him was the promise. Nations are today blessed in Abraham by covenant.

In the process of growing up, Esau, coming from

the fields, found his young brother having prepared red soup. Hungry and appetized, Esau was ready to purchase the soup. He was ready to make covenant and move from being elder, giving way to the younger, provided Jacob would give him the much adored soup in return. This was unsupervised by any of their parents. We cannot blame either father or mother for this transaction. The twins seemed to understand covenant more than we ever think. This should not come as a surprise considering the young men lived in a covenant family. Their parents were covenant people. It must be that covenant was spoken of and taught in the house. When Esau agreed in principle to sell his birthright, Jacob demanded that big brother swore it and he obliged. If this was child play, why swear? Who was a child after all? Esau coming from the fields or from a hunting trip could not be as young as we imagine. If he could deal with lions, hyenas and bears alone in the wilderness and fell large animals for meat to bring home, was he still the child in your mind? *(Gen 25:27) And the boys grew: and Esau was a cunning hunter, a man of the field; and Jacob was a plain man, dwelling in tents*.

Esau offered to buy and Jacob accepted to supply the soup at a birthright price. Jacob honoured his obligation in the sale by supplying the goods; the soup as ordered by the buyer, Esau. He received   and surely partook of this soup. There and then Jacob became Isaac's eldest son, although the father was not made aware of it. The brothers had come of age and could make their own decisions. Already you can see that Jacob became Isaac's first born son and would be blessed accordingly. Something worrying was Esau's lack of respect for his position. He did not care about his birthright at all. He seemed to think that since they were only minutes different in age, there was nothing to write home about being first born at all. Do not blame the mother, she was not there. The boys were on their own. How would Esau despise his birthright like that? Why did his mind not wake up or his heart beat when his brother demanded him to sign the agreement by swearing? Did he think he was cheating Jacob? If so, then who was the cheat and crook between the two?

When you hear him speaking for the soup against his birthright, you will agree he was not the one for it. He despised all about being the elder brother and praised the red soup which he demanded must be given to him as the birthright did not matter according to him. He said it was of no use. He did not need it, so did not deserve it. Exalting soup above it, Esau lost the crucial birthright. *(Gen 25:33) And Jacob said, Swear to me this day. And he swore to him, and he sold his birthright to Jacob. (Gen 25:34) Then Jacob gave Esau bread and soup of lentils. And he ate and drank, and rose up and went his way. And Esau despised his birthright*. Now, the birthright had fallen into the hands of him who valued it and seemed to understand its meaning. While Esau let go the birthright for soup, Jacob let go the soup for the birthright. Their thinking patterns were just that opposite. Before we bring God into the story, the twins had a deal. Esau should have said 'No Deal' if he was for the birthright.

Examining Esau's life, we find there are some issues which themselves could disqualify him from ascending to the position he so much desired despite having cashed in on it. His parents had been made miserable by his marriages. The parents were totally grieved right into the spirit by the wives, Hittite wives of Esau. *(Gen 26:34) And Esau was forty years old when he took to wife Judith the daughter of Beeri the Hittite, and Basemath the daughter of Elon the Hittite;(Gen 26:35) who were a grief of spirit to Isaac and to Rebekah*. Isaac and his wife were grieving in the spirit due to their son's two wives. This was very dangerous as it went down to their spirit which could on its own trigger a fall out as Isaac was to bless from the spirit *(Gen 27:4).* It hurt both the parents so much that Isaac had to call Jacob, commanding him to go seek a wife for himself by Laban's place and never to marry in his brother Esau's footsteps. According to Isaac, Esau had already failed covenant values by bringing in wrong wives from outside acceptable boarders while their behaviour was grossly distressing to the aging parents.

Rebekah, the mother of the twins, is also under fire by the modern day Christians. They accuse her of orchestrating a coup by Jacob which resultantly overthrew the big brother from the birthright throne. Well thought, but there is need to look closer and see if she is accusable without implicating God lest we find ourselves in danger of mocking Him. *(Gal 6:7) Do not be deceived, God is not mocked...* It was not about the mother, but about God whose plan it was to empower the barren woman to conceive and have such type of twins whose war began right from the womb. They knew what they were fighting for. God who plans and appoints people before they depart from their mother's wombs had already made His appointment. Any attempts to wrestle with God's plans would only prove futile. *(Jer 1:5) "Before I formed you in the womb I knew you, and before you were born I consecrated you; I appointed you a prophet to the nations."*

It is worth our while to note that many of the men of God were called from barren wombs. The mothers were barren. Samuel's mother was barren, Samson's mother was barren. Sarah, Isaac's mother was barren and now Isaac's wife was also barren. God has a way of working from scratch to cause His will to come out perfect. Isaac prayed for his barren wife and God opened her womb *(Gen 25:21).* The result is that God becomes involved right from conception. In this case, you could safely say this pregnancy was a result of prayer. Isaac had prayed for his wife to conceive. I wish many men could do the same today instead of just blaming their wives for not conceiving when it may not even be known who in the marriage has the shortcoming. Rebekah knew that it was through prayer that she had become fertile. When she found there was war inside her womb she simply returned to Him who had empowered her to overcome barrenness. She went back to God and requested an explanation. It is clear the woman spoke to God and God spoke to this woman. She walked with God throughout this pregnancy, God talking to her plainly and not in dreams. We want to guess what she should or should not have done, but she did not guess any of it. She heard straight from God. To put it more accurately, she discussed it with God. Her actions cannot be contested by us as we base our argument on thoughts and imaginations while hers is on what she heard and saw from God the Almighty.

It was God who educated her on the complicities of the pregnancy; who was in the womb and who was to be whom. She was told in black and white who was to take lead. She also had seen Jacob come out with his hand pulling the heel of Esau. All this would confirm what God had told her about the twins who God called 'nations' and 'peoples' in her womb. No one else can explain God's plans for the boys more than Rebekah who heard from and spoke with God on this matter from the beginning. Not even Isaac could challenge his wife on this one. He knew that his wife had found favour with the Lord.

Looking at the dynamics surroundings the birth of the most famous twins of all time, Esau and Jacob, an interesting question can be put forward; did Esau come out first? Do we have a clear one after another delivery capable of separating the first from the second? I do not think so. If the hand of Jacob came out holding the heel of Esau, we may have had a continuous act of delivery where you are drawn into thinking this was a single delivery where neither could claim a higher birth right. Just leave this aside and accept Jacob of God as the one holding the blessing of the birthright now.

Chapter Three

The Moment of Blessing

et's approach the most popular event in the history of the twins. The moment of blessing! We need to understand how the actual blessing took place and how it was sustained later in scripture. We learn that Isaac called his beloved son Esau to brief him on the blessings. He instructed him to prepare for him his favourite dish which was game meat. Esau needed to go hunt then come and prepare it and give beloved father who was to eat to his satisfaction and in turn bless his supposedly first born son before dying. At this point Isaac's eyes had grown dim with age and he could only identify his two sons by voice or touching and feeling. It was easy for him as he knew their voices pretty well and the differences of their hands as Esau was hairy while Jacob was smooth. He would not mistake Esau's voice as he spent more time with his favourite son than with Jacob. *(Gen 25:28) And Isaac loved Esau, for game was in his mouth.*

So here we go; Isaac calls Esau and begins to tell him confidentially that he would bless him as soon as he brought his favourite dish of hunted game. Mother Rebekah is vigilantly listening and her mind captures what is about to happen. She recalls her conversations with God. Remember, what is bound on earth is also bound in heaven. The two brothers had one thing they had bound on earth which Esau was willing to forget and yet heavens were not. It was the exchange of birth positions. The mother has heard the conversation. Give the woman a break; if God did not hide from her the secret of the two nations; were Isaac and son Esau going to succeed? Any God fearing person would have done what Rebekah did if at all it would emerge that the time for God's word to be fulfilled had come and you were favoured to play a part.

It may be that some people may not know the impact of hearing when God speaks. It was not only God's word but also His voice. There is a good difference between 'word' and 'voice'. While word includes what was spoken or written through others, the 'voice' refers to actual direct active personal live speaking which includes volume, tone, emphasis, mood, breath and authority at times favoured with appearance. Try and imagine yourself actually hearing the voice of the Lord! We are on earth to fulfil the Lord's plans and not ours. I know someone may want to say the woman should not have tried to assist God for His will should have fallen in place by divine power. Very well put, but then why are we all preaching the gospel today? Why don't we leave God's will to prevail on its own so that all people will just repent without our participation lest we be found assisting God? We are vessels of God which can be used at any time at the pleasure of Him who plans all things for His great purposes. Why was Moses saved in a basket by someone? Why didn't God find His own divine way of bringing Moses into Egypt and sustain him until the appointed hour? God did exactly that by using those people who took him into the palace. Elijah had to be fed by a widow who God had put in place for that purpose. God works with people. It is for our good that God works this way. Didn't the widow get saved from the famine just by feeding the prophet of the Lord? It took courage for Rahab the harlot to house the Israelite delegation in Jericho. She had to be there to facilitate the spying mission. God put her there in the same way He put Rebekah in a place to facilitate the performance of His will. Was the household of Rahab not spared when she was instructed to put a scarlet on her house? Mary was present at the wedding at Cana and she told people to do whatever Jesus told them and a miracle of good wine happened. *(Joh 2:5) His mother said to the servants, "Do whatever he tells you."* Why didn't Jesus do it without his mother? God used Mary to prepare people for the miracle. In the subject case God used Jacob's mother to get him into the position He wanted him to be.

It is not like God would fail to do whatever He wishes without people. He can do all things without needing us and yet we cannot do without needing Him. Examples do abound of how God did many things without people from creation to this day. He once commanded ravens to feed Elijah and caused a donkey to speak back to Balaam. We know how He fed the Israelites with manna and quails and how he parted the red sea. Even though Moses played a part, he did not build walls to part the waters. God did it by an all-night wind. In the New Testament, we see God bringing out Paul and Silas from Prison. The same happened to Peter who was led out by an angel. The Lord caused the death of Herod who burst into worms as he spoke against God and His people. Another popular one is about Saul, now Paul, on his journey to Damascus where he was stricken off the horse and warned not to kick against pricks. Saul turned blind for a while.

However, if God continues to work on His own, then our purpose on earth is nullified. He works with us for our own sake to create purpose and fulfilment in us thereby causing us to believe. God uses men as well as women. The bible is full of chronicles of people who were used by God to make things work according to His design. Even Jesus had to be hidden from Herod by people. Could we ask why they were helping God? They were not helping God at all. They were fulfilling a calling. God loves working with people. This also creates record of God's work on earth. If we just woke up and found curious things having happened where there was no one witnessing, how would we know it was God? For this purpose God put us on earth, that we may represent His Kingdom here. Some may want to ask why God chose Jacob instead of Esau. It is just as lame as asking why that mountain is in Russia instead of Canada. God has His own ways. Trust Him. To try and look at it from another angle, do you not see that God foresaw how irresponsible Esau would be and decided to protect His covenant by skipping him in the process? Just imagine the consequences if Esau had sold the birthright or the blessing to a total stranger. How many things would Esau have disposed of whenever he felt hungry and to who? When you look at it from that point of view, you will agree that the Lord who knows us before we are born did not see Esau as a good steward and as such He saw it a better loss for the birthright to be exchanged within the same household than for it ending up in the hands of God's enemies.

God knew what He was doing. Am I making your reading enjoyable at all or is it becoming more complicated? I know you love God and you believe His plans are good and that we do not see all things as plainly as God does or as we ought. We are limited to what we can physically see or feel or even hear. The rest, only God understands. The good thing is that it always works well and for the good.

Moving back to the moment of blessing, Isaac called Esau to tell him about the blessings which could only be conferred upon him after feeding game to the father. The conversation was divinely heard by Rebekah and the obvious happened. She, as an informed person alerted the rightful person to act. She was the woman of God around and took care of God's business*. (Gen 27:1) When Isaac was old and his eyes were dim so that he could not see, he called Esau his older son and said to him, "My son"; and he answered, "Here*

I am."(Gen 27:2) He said, "Behold, I am old; I do not know the day of my death. (Gen 27:3) Now then, take your weapons, your quiver and your bow, and go out to the field and hunt game for me, (Gen 27:4) and prepare for me delicious food, such as I love, and bring it to me so that I may eat, that my soul may bless you before I die."(Gen 27:5) Now Rebekah was listening when Isaac spoke to his son Esau. So when Esau went to the field to hunt for game and bring it,(Gen 27:6) Rebekah said to her son Jacob, "I heard your father speak to your brother Esau,(Gen 27:7) 'Bring me game and prepare for me delicious food, that I may eat it and bless you before the LORD before I die.'(Gen 27:8) Now therefore, my son, obey my voice as I command you. (Gen 27:9) Go to the flock and bring me two good young goats, so that I may prepare from them delicious food for your father, such as he loves. (Gen 27:10) And you shall bring it to your father to eat, so that he may bless you before he dies."

I like Jacob's response to his mother's plan. After being told by his mother to go and say he was Esau and receive a blessing from his nearly blind father, Jacob told her he feared being cursed and would not do it. Can you see that if Jacob was not the rightful person, he would have ended up with a curse instead of a blessing? Rebekah, knowing how God had authored what was about to happen, told her son confidently that if there be any case she would take it herself instead of Jacob. She was not afraid at all. Clearly, she knew it was the right thing to do. It's also worth our while noting from the scripture that Jacob hated being a deceiver. *(Gen 27:12) My father will perhaps feel me, and I shall seem to him as a deceiver. And I shall bring a curse upon me, and not a blessing. (Gen 27:13) And his mother said to him, Your curse be upon me, my son, only obey my voice and go bring them to me*.

'Only obey my voice my son', said the mother. Why her voice? She obviously was telling her son she was not astray but all was in order and hers was the correct way to do it. It may be that the Lord had instructed her to act this way or she knew and understood from prior conversations with the Lord that this was the right thing for her to do. No curse was to come upon her or her son Jacob. Isaac proceeded to bless him despite noticing that the voice was not Esau's but Jacob's. When sight is lost, the other senses become stronger so that more can be achieved through hearing, feeling or even smelling in a compensatory manner. He would have relied on hearing more than feeling as he, without any doubt, would be so acquainted to their voices and yet he proceeded to bless a person whose voice he knew was not Esau's.

The aging father even mentioned that the voice was not Esau's. *(Gen 27:22) And Jacob went near to Isaac his father. And he felt him and said, The voice is Jacob's voice*. What was happening? When Esau came in just after Jacob had left, Isaac was categorical clear there was no way of reversing the blessing. Jacob earlier had told his mother that if it was wrong, a curse would follow; meaning on realization, the father would reverse the blessing and curse him instead. It was not to be. Isaac actually confirmed the blessing by telling Esau he could not reverse anything and that he had made Jacob lord over him. *(Gen 27:37) Isaac answered and said to Esau, "Behold, I have made him lord over you, and all his brothers I have given to him for servants, and with grain and wine I have sustained him. What then can I do for you, my son?"* Isaac had no anger or feeling of a cheated father. It was not like Isaac died immediately after the blessing incident that we may think there was no time for him to reverse the blessing. He only died after the return of Jacob from twenty years in Haran and was buried by both his twin sons. *(Gen 35:29) And Isaac breathed his last and died, and was gathered to his people, old and satisfied of days. And his sons, Esau and Jacob, buried him.*

Surely the Lord had given Abraham's seed both to bless and to curse respectively. It was up to Isaac to curse or to bless. So why did he not curse Jacob and put things right by blessing Esau if at all Jacob had cheated? Jacob had not cheated. Only Esau felt the pain and thought he had been cheated when he, in fact, had feasted on the soup in a daylight exchange. Esau's anger was both against his brother and himself as he regretted the soup and birthright exchange and how he was facing the drastic consequences. He hated the day of the soup.

Esau began to breathe anger and sought opportunity to kill his twin, now elder brother, Jacob. Rebekah was once again well placed to hear the gossip of the planned murder. If not by divine appointment, why was she always there to hear things before hand while there still was time to take remedial action? She hurriedly planned for her now first born son Jacob to escape to Haran where her brother Laban dwelt. The newly crowned first born son was to remain there until Esau's anger had subsided. *(Gen 27:41) Now Esau hated Jacob because of the blessing with which his father had blessed him and Esau said to himself, "The days of mourning for my father are approaching; then I will kill my brother Jacob."(Gen 27:42) But the words of Esau her elder son were told to Rebekah. So she sent and called Jacob her younger son and said to him, "Behold, your brother Esau comforts himself about you by planning to kill you. (Gen 27:43) Now therefore, my son, obey my voice. Arise; flee to Laban my brother in Haran.*

Rebekah, in seeking refuge for her son would soon introduce a good story to Isaac and remind him how unhappy they had been with Esau's Hittite wives; a kind of marriage their son Jacob should never fall into. Soon Isaac was on the story to get Jacob to Haran to choose a wife. There had been genuine sorrow brought upon the elderly couple by their son Esau's Hittite wives. Look at it again*. (Gen 26:34) When Esau was forty years old, he took Judith the daughter of Beeri the Hittite to be his wife, and Basemath the daughter of Elon the Hittite, (Gen 26:35) and they made life bitter for Isaac and Rebekah*.

It looks like Isaac and Rebekah felt relieved the right person had been blessed. They immediately discussed their sorrow at the hands of the Hittite wives of Esau. Isaac felt he would get it done right this time by instructing Jacob never to marry in the footsteps of his brother Esau. He called Jacob and blessed him again, this time without anyone coming in someone's name and instructed the newly blessed Jacob to go and marry within Laban's family.

Isaac blessed Jacob over and over again as if to celebrate God's plan. He then sent him away to Laban's *(Gen 28:6).* It immediately dawned to Esau that his parents had never been happy with his wives when he heard them telling Jacob not to marry such women commanding him to go and marry from the house of Laban his mother's brother. We see Esau trying to mend this by himself going to marry a non Hittite third wife. *(Gen 28:6) Now Esau saw that Isaac had blessed Jacob and sent him away to Paddan-aram to take a wife from there, and that as he blessed him he directed him, "You must not take a wife from the Canaanite women," (Gen 28:7) and that Jacob had obeyed his father and his mother and gone to Paddan-aram. (Gen 28:8) So when Esau saw that the Canaanite women did not please Isaac his father, (Gen 28:9) Esau went to Ishmael and took as his wife, besides the wives he had, Mahalath the daughter of Ishmael, Abraham's son, the sister of Nebaioth*.

Isaac and Rebekah seemed openly happy with the

developments concerning their son Jacob. God was never to be the God of Esau but the God of Jacob. When He appeared to Moses at Mt Horeb, God told him without hesitation, He was the God of Abraham, Isaac and Jacob. God said it Himself. Do you think even God was cheated by Jacob? Obviously God did not partake of the red soup. He was not cheated or bought by Jacob. God chose Jacob. Rebekah worked to fulfil God's plan like every committed woman and man of God would do today. What do you understand when God says He loved Jacob and not Esau? Where do people come in when God is clearly declaring His choice? *(Mal 1:2)...Was not Esau Jacob's brother, saith Jehovah: yet I loved Jacob; (Mal 1:3) but Esau I hated*.

Many of us have just spoken against Jacob from simple innocence of ignorance. Even the only piece of scripture *(Hos 12:2)* that may sound to say something unpleasant does not seem to say what we think it does about him. Even if it might, the intention of God is assessed from comparing the frequency of scripture on the subject in which case the whole bible goes on to demonstrate that God chose Jacob over Esau without further indications that God ever blamed Rebekah or Jacob for turning over the tables because they did not. Where the Lord declares, 'Jacob I loved, Esau I hated', do we still hold any argument?

Chapter Four

To Haran with God

J acob started his journey to Haran. While on the surface it was like Jacob was retreating from Esau to go into hiding in Padden-aram, Haran, it was his father's wish that prevailed. Isaac wanted Jacob to marry there. While it is correctly announced that Jacob was running away from Esau, it was the will of his father that was being fulfilled. *(Gen 28:2) Arise, go to Padanaram, to the house of Bethuel your mother's father. And take a wife from there of the daughters of Laban your mother's brother*. According to Isaac, Jacob was in   pursuit of a marriage. You can see that there are times when it's like we are in trouble and yet we are on course to accomplish other important things. What people see may not be what God is doing with you. They will only be surprised when your uplifted position is revealed.

The Lord did not leave Jacob alone in all this. In fact, this situation would create a wonderful opportunity for Jacob to rub shoulders with the Lord. In the middle of darkness, alone on the journey, the sun having set, he prepared to sleep on the way. Turning a stone into a pillow, he slept but he was not alone. The Lord was following him. At this time he had his first encounter with God who was not at all angry with him. God was following the blessed man to fulfil His promises, not to rebuke him for stealing someone's blessings. We would have thought God was to start by asking Jacob of the blessings. We should probably have expected Jacob to hear a loud fierce voice of rebuke asking him 'what do you think you are doing, running away with your brother's birthright? Do you consider yourself very clever?'. No, not at all! God looks at things from His own perspective and not from our less informed angle. God was following the first born son of Isaac to fulfil the promises on the seed of Abraham. Do not get confused when I say first born son because Jacob was now. God arrived with a promise of better things. Dreaming of a ladder joining heaven and earth, Jacob saw the Lord standing on the ladder pronouncing upon him promises. If Jacob was not the rightful person, what is God doing with him? I would not think we are more righteous than God who does not see a crook in Jacob but a father of nations. *(Gen 28:12) And he dreamed, and behold, there was a ladder set up on the earth, and the top of it reached to heaven. And behold, the angels of God were ascending and descending on it! (Gen 28:13) And behold, the LORD stood above it and said, "I am the LORD, the God of Abraham your father and the God of Isaac. The land on which you lie I will give to you and to your offspring. (Gen 28:14) Your offspring shall be like the dust of the earth, and you shall spread abroad to the west and to the east and to the north and to the south, and in you and your offspring shall all the families of the earth be blessed. (Gen 28:15) Behold, I am with you and will keep you wherever you go, and will bring you back to this land. For I will not leave you until I have done what I have promised you."*

While we think Jacob was just running away, we find he was moving in God's plan. It became the first time Jacob was alone in the wild where his brother Esau had spent most of his time hunting and never had an encounter with God. It was Jacob's first opportunity to be away from his mother. He was mum's boy who knew nothing about outdoor life. This is the time God was looking for in order to talk to him and announce to him that the land on which he was standing would be possessed by his offspring. If anyone was mocking Jacob for going to take refuge, they would soon envy him. The Lord had no other story with the now first born son of Isaac but to keep reminding him he was not alone and was blessed and that his offspring would possess the land. God also was going to be with him where ever he was going and promised to bring him back. When you look at these facts, who do you think is better off now between Esau, left in the comfort of a home, and Jacob who is moving alone in the wilderness with God on his side? You can see that the life of this man is well surrounded by the Lord and His promises. God appears to him and encourages him so that he does not lose his confidence over events at home. No better thing would one ever wish for than having fellowship with God at such a time! With God's promise that He was going to be with him, Jacob continued his journey to Haran. Clearly, his fear was now a thing of the past, for one man with God is majority. There is no indication that God was angry in any way. God's announcements are all covenant fulfilling. God seems so pleased with the success of the birthright transfer that He keeps appearing and assuring and reassuring Jacob of His protection, favour and blessings.

We are soon to find out that no evil ever befell Jacob on his way. Nothing to indicate he was on the wrong! No attacks from thieves, no illness and not even an encounter with dangerous wild animals! His journey was completely safe with God the only visitor time after time. I say this was a memorable time in the life of this man. Suggesting that Jacob is a thief by his mother's design can really complicate things and implicate God. We may not want to find ourselves in the same situation as some of the Palestinians, the Iranians and any of the radical worlds who continuously contest the legitimacy of Israel. Every time we condemn Jacob, we are like these people, ignorant of God's will and plan. You need to see the glory of God in how His will was implemented. How brothers could have their positions swapped in favour of the will and design of God must be a reason for us to see the glory and the greatness of the Lord. Any approach to the contrary puts us in danger of mocking God knowing very well it is Him who said the elder would serve the younger. *(Gal 6:7)* *Do not be deceived: God is not mocked.*

Chapter Five

Jacob's Turn

When his turn to pass blessings came we find Jacob doing the same with Joseph's sons. He blessed the younger instead of the elder. Despite Joseph's efforts to remind him to bless the elder, Jacob proceeded to bless the younger declaring he knew what he was doing for it was the younger that was to be greater. Though his eyes had grown deem, Jacob clearly declared he knew he was blessing the younger as it was meant to be so. This, done with full knowledge, without anyone pretending names, shows that even Isaac did the same on Esau and Jacob. So Ephraim was blessed in the place of his elder brother Manasseh. No mothers involved! *(Gen 48:14) And Israel stretched out his right hand and laid it on the head of Ephraim, who was the younger, and his left hand on the head of Manasseh, crossing his hands (for Manasseh was the firstborn). (Gen 48:15) And he blessed Joseph and said, "The God before whom my fathers Abraham and Isaac walked, the God who has been my shepherd all my life long to this day, (Gen 48:16) the angel who has redeemed me from all evil, bless the boys; and in them let my name be carried on, and the name of my fathers Abraham and Isaac;*

and let them grow into a multitude in the midst of the earth." (Gen 48:17) When Joseph saw that his father laid his right hand on the head of Ephraim, it displeased him, and he took his father's hand to move it from Ephraim's head to Manasseh's head. (Gen 48:18) And Joseph said to his father, "Not this way, my father; since this one is the firstborn, put your right hand on his head." (Gen 48:19) But his father refused and said, "I know, my son, I know. He also shall become a people, and he also shall be great. Nevertheless, his younger brother shall be greater than he, and his offspring shall become a multitude of nations."

What is interesting is that the boys had been brought by their father Joseph to their grandfather Jacob in the correct order for the right hand to fall on the elder but Jacob went as far as crossing his hands. His eyes deem as they had become as he was about to die, he still could divinely feel where his grandson Ephraim was and crossed his hands to follow and bless the younger in place of the elder. Joseph who was not very acquainted with this way of doing things, pulled his father's hand from the younger directing him to bless the elder, only to be silenced when Jacob said he knew but he would bless the younger as he would be greater than the elder.

It is very clear that God has His ways of doing things and it does not help much for us to try and put our carnal thoughts to it. This also goes to show that it is not in being born first, otherwise the whole process would remain natural and canal. It is a good sign that God will work with anyone He chooses regardless of whom they are or their history. Remember the covenant between Abraham and God was not based on the law which was not yet written but on faith thereby making Abraham the father of faith. This would later show that whosoever would believe in God would be accepted Jew or not, first born, middle or last. Abraham is the father or even the founder of faith. He believed God and that was taken as righteousness. *(Gal 3:6)...Abraham believed God, and it was accounted to him for righteousness*. God's way had to prevail. We all need to understand that God will choose whoever He will and it can never be up to us to contest that regardless of how much we may disapprove of that choice. God's thoughts will continue to differ from ours. We will never come to a point where we can ever claim to know everything about God's ways. *(Isa 55:8) For My thoughts are not your thoughts, nor your ways My ways, says Jehovah. (Isa 55:9) For as the heavens are higher than the earth, so are My ways higher than your ways, and My thoughts than your thoughts.*

The journey and protocol of these blessings continue to be beyond human calculation. We can talk of so many people who ended up involved although they may have seemed remote. What do you say about Solomon the son of David? Did he not have elder brothers? Is not his mother the former wife of Uriah? Did he not become king? His elder brother Adonijah who unsuccessfully tried to ascend to the throne later admitted that Solomon had the throne given to him by the Lord. *(1Ki 2:15) And Adonijah said, You know that the kingdom was mine, and that all Israel set their faces on me that I should reign. However, the kingdom is turned around, and has become my brother's. For it was his from Jehovah.* Does Jesus not hail from Solomon's linage? You can find people like Rahab the harlot in Jesus' genealogy and a few other 'undeserving' names if the scale was ours. We may think some protocol was broken many times as the Lord's will prevailed. Until this day, it is the Lord's will that creates the state of Israel despite fierce resistance by some who try to follow genealogies without understanding the will and plan of God. Once Israel was given the land by God, it became his and his seed's despite any existing ownership records and history that may compel to the contrary. Jacob did not steal this land, did he? Was it not promised by God to Abraham and later on confirmed to Jacob? We all know it was. It was and is still called the Promised Land. This is not contestable. The best we can do is to love Jerusalem and pray for its peace so we can prosper. *(Psa 122:6) Pray for the peace of Jerusalem: they shall prosper that love thee.* Jacob arrived in Haran safely as promised by God who had sworn to be with Him in every place he went until His will was fulfilled. In a short while he was in the house of Laban where things began to happen in mixed ways. Once Jacob laid his hands on Laban's work, everything began to change. Laban saw a marked difference in everything of his as Jacob's blessed hands brought him success. In a short while Jacob was to find himself with the wrong woman. After working for seven years to have Rachel as his wife, it was Leah who ended up on his bed. All these were Laban's tricks for his gain. So now, where does it show that Jacob cheated Laban? Is it not Laban who cheated Jacob? *(Gen 29:25) And in the morning, behold, it was Leah! And Jacob said to Laban, "What is this you have done to me? Did I not serve with you for Rachel? Why then have you deceived me?*

May the Lord's Holy Spirit help us to understand simple things when we read His word! While he thought he was taking advantage of Jacob, Laban did not know that anything concerning Jacob would only happen if it furthered the purpose of the Kingdom of God, for Leah then mothered Judah and it is in his linage that Jesus was born. Rachel was later given to Jacob who would then work another seven years for her father Laban in return. This was all crookedly planned by Laban so he could benefit from the man's blessed labour and secure the future of his daughters. Clearly Jacob is the victim here, only God continues to raise him to victor. Do you still blame Jacob? What else would you have to point your finger at?

Laban still refused Jacob exit after serving for the second wife for he said he would not let Jacob go as he was being blessed because of him*. (Gen 30:26) Give me my wives and my children, for whom I have served thee, and let me go: for thou knowest my service which I have done thee. (Gen 30:27) And Laban said* *unto him, I pray thee, if I have found favour in thine eyes, tarry: for I have learned by experience that the LORD hath blessed me for thy sake*.

Laban devised to pay Jacob in an agreed way. Every spotted and speckled sheep were to belong to Jacob. Laban agreed but went in and removed all spotted and speckled sheep and put them in charge of his sons without Jacob's knowledge. Once again the question, who was cheating who? It still comes openly clear that Laban is doing the evil. Do you still blame Jacob? What else did he have to do to appeal to your conscience? He was the victim throughout were it not for God with whom he had a covenant for protection and a partnership that covered his wealth for which tithes would be paid when all was over.

Laban's actions did not help him but only left Jacob with no choice but to invoke the power of Him who was with him and change things. Jacob later put sticks with peeled sides in the well in a way that caused all those breeding to bring out offspring that was spotted and speckled causing Jacob's flock to grow bigger than that of Laban. *(Gen 31:11) Then the angel of God said to me in the dream, 'Jacob,' and I said, 'Here I am!'(Gen 31:12) And he said, 'Lift up your eyes and see, all the goats that mate with the flock are striped, spotted, and mottled, for I have seen all that Laban is doing to you.*

One cannot insist that Jacob defrauded Laban without implicating God Himself and the angel that He sent to direct Jacob, to place the peeled sticks in the well in order to influence the colour of the animals that would be born thereafter. If anybody ever thinks Jacob just placed sticks and, without God's anointing, the offspring of the sheep changed, then let them try at home and see if sticks work without God. Jacob had been cheated probably more times than recorded. How many times? We do not know but here is an estimate from the victim himself. *(Gen 31:7) yet your father has cheated me and changed my wages ten times. But God did not permit him to harm me*. Jacob did not steal from Laban. God only interfered to level the unlevelled playing field. God protected Jacob's earnings because he had promised to do so and that is what He does when we pay our tithes. Remember Jacob was going to pay a tithe of all according to his vow to the Lord. Accordingly, if Jacob succeeded then God succeeded. Jacob could not labour in vain. God forbade that as Jacob was His partner in all things including wealth. Let's look at the vow once more and see how Jacob promises to pay tithes. *(Gen 28:22)... "And of all that you give me I will give a full tenth to you."* What is interesting is that God would receive a full tenth, without deductions, of all He was to give to Jacob away from home. What is a full tenth? Certainly, it is a tenth as one out of ten or ten out of a hundred proportionately without excuses or deductions. The first to give is God, and then we have to learn to give back just a tenth as a sign of trusting that He will give us again. Remember you did not have until He gave you. I do not get where the problem is in giving to

Him who gave you first so He can give you again, even more. When you do not give Him back, it's not His loss but yours as you may not expect Him to trust and give you again. **Malachi Chapter three** explains how God will protect your wealth by stopping the devourer and the moth if you pay tithes. On the same scripture God promises to open the windows of heaven.

Can you see that all that Jacob worked for was about to be devoured? Laban and sons were plotting to attack Jacob but they could not. God actually came by night and warned Laban that Jacob was untouchable. *(Gen 31:24) And God came to Laban the Syrian in a dream by night, and said to him, Take heed that you do not speak either good or bad to Jacob*. Laban tried in vain to cheat Jacob. No one can cheat you in any way if you are in partnership with the Lord. They can only cheat themselves but not you. Any evil plan hatched against you will only backfire against the plotters. I want you to understand that Jacob took nothing by false pretences or violence. God calculated Jacob's worth and gave him from Laban's flock. Also worthy to remember is that God takes the wealth of the wicked and allocates to those who fear His name. Whatever Jacob got was given to him by the Lord (*Gen 31:9) Thus God has taken away the livestock of your father and given them to me*.

Chapter Six

Back to Father's House

J acob became so wealthy that Laban's sons grew jealousy and complained bitterly to their father as they felt Jacob had taken everything that belonged to them, leaving them without any inheritance. At the instruction of an angel, Jacob left Laban's place wealthier than Laban. Remember he had come with nothing but just a staff, not even a pillow as he had to use a stone for one. In due course the Lord remembered covenant and told Jacob it was high time he returned to his father's house. God was anxious to fulfil His word by taking Jacob back alive, well and wealthy, which He did. God remembered Jacob's vow and reassured him it was time to go and that the agreement was still on. Nobody could stop him. God had not forgotten the vow. *(Gen 31:13) I am the God of Bethel, where you anointed a pillar and made a vow to me. Now arise, go out from this land and return to the land of your kindred."*

Clearly, it was God who initiated Jacob's escape from Laban when it became clear that his life was now in danger after Laban's countenance had changed towards him. Laban could not stop Jacob although he followed him and his wives and children. God was with Jacob according to the promise, even warning Laban against touching Jacob. Let's look at this again. *(Gen 31:24) And God came to Laban the Syrian in a dream of the night, and said unto him, Take heed to thyself that thou speak not to Jacob either good or bad.* At this point God was busy fulfilling His promise to bring Jacob back to his father's house safe. Jacob came back substantially wealthy.

He soon was to make peace with Esau, this becoming the most important victory in his life so far. It would only be after wrestling with an unknown man, referred to by scripture as God who had appeared unto him and Jacob refused to let go besides His appeals as the sun was rising. Jacob insisted on a blessing and there, his name was changed from Jacob to Israel for the man said Jacob had fought with men and God and prevailed. *(Gen 32:28) Then he said, "Your name shall no longer be called Jacob, but Israel, for you have striven with God and with men, and have prevailed."*

Jacob had wrestled with a heavenly being which left him limping after taking out his hip from the socket. *(Gen 32:25) When the man saw that he did not prevail against Jacob, he touched his hip socket, and Jacob's hip was put out of joint as he wrestled with him.*

This is so real an experience and not a dream so that even to this day the children of Israel do not eat sinews from the thigh of any animal because of their father's hip encounter with God. *(Gen 32:32) Therefore the sons of Israel do not eat of the sinew of the thigh, which is on the hip-socket, until this day, because He touched Jacob's hip-socket, the sinew of the thigh.*

So far, the greatest victory for Jacob was his emotional reunion with Esau without any battle although Esau had approached his returning twin brother with four hundred men. The Lord had surely been faithful in taking Jacob to Haran and bringing him back to his father's house safe and wealthy. It is important to note that, although Jacob's name was changed to Israel, God continued to call Himself the God of Abraham, Isaac and Jacob. God did not refer himself much as the God of Israel but of Jacob. This may be because Israel was Jacob's multiplication name yet Jacob was the name describing the battle for the birthright. Contrary to popular believe, there was nothing wrong with the name 'Jacob' which only explains how he came out of the womb holding his brothers heel. While there are other translations to this name, this particular one was given as an explanation of clutching the heel. In another dictionary the same name means 'Protected of God'. I doubt if this refers to this particular one. God seems to like this name; it may be because it explains the battle from the womb.

Jacob became Israel and his offspring is known by this name until this day. God chose to be called 'The God of Abraham, Isaac and Jacob'. Blessed is he who blesses Israel (Jacob*). (Num 24:9)... Blessed is he who blesses you, and cursed is he who curses you.*

Chapter Seven

In Defence of Jacob

Clearly, Jacob cannot be cursed. This does not necessarily mean God does not have issues with Jacob, called Israel. Even when God has something to shout at Israel for, it is not to be misunderstood for an open ground for all to do the same. Any dispute will remain domestic between God and His man of covenant while the promise remains in force that whoever curses Jacob, also called Israel, will surely be cursed of God and whoever blesses him will be blessed.

Let's visit this one; *(Num 22:28) Then the Lord opened the mouth of the donkey, and she said to Balaam, "What have I done to you, that you have struck me these three times?"* Wow, can you believe it? You have no choice because it happened. The donkey spoke with its own mouth. Why? There must be something that had angered God beyond the norm in order for Him to break natural laws and give the donkey a mouth to speak like this. Tell me, did you ever dream of a donkey talking one day? I didn't and I don't think you did. The unexpected did happen. Even angels began to run up and down the heaven and the earth to see how they could stand for and with Israel. God's rage was kindled in defence of Israel. That is how jealous God is about Jacob. He was so enraged Balaam had accepted an invitation to go and curse Israel and in the hurry to defend His people, the donkey ended up with its mouth open to talk.

God was ready to do whatever it took in defence of Jacob. The children of Israel were not even aware of the plot by the king of Moab and yet God took notice. God watches over Israel. That is what happens to God's loved ones. Even though we may be unaware of conspiracies, curses and wars brewing somewhere against us, our God will deal with all that on our behalf. Jesus promised that He would be with us to the end. He remains the author and finisher of our faith. Remember when Stephen was being stoned, Jesus Christ who is normally seated at the right hand of the Father actually stood up. We hear the scripture saying: *(Act 7:55) But he, full of the Holy Spirit, gazed into heaven and saw the glory of God, and Jesus standing at the right hand of God*. Jesus, the commander of the armed forces of heaven stood up in defence of His man. Well, presented with a choice, Steven gave up the ghost after seeing the glory up there. He was not killed neither did he just die. He gave up the ghost. *(Act 7:59) And as they were stoning Stephen, he called out, "Lord Jesus, receive my spirit."*

During his journey, the donkey upon which Balaam rode began to behave strangely. This prompted Balaam to smite it and there the donkey opened its mouth and spoke telling Balaam there was an Angel who could have killed him had the donkey not swayed and even lay down to save him and yet he was ignorant of all that was happening. The donkey put him to task and asked him how long he had ridden on it for and if ever it had once behaved this way at any time before. Can you notice donkeys now speak for the first time on record and an angel moving to want to strike Balaam because he has embarked on a journey to curse the children of Israel? Why? It is simple. Nobody will be left to curse Israel. Looking at it, the main story is not about the donkey opening its mouth to speak but about a man and his offspring who cannot be cursed, to the extent that even a donkey will speak when God is jealoused up to save His own. Balaam had been summoned by the king of Moab, Balak, to go and stand his corner and curse Israel who was approaching on the way from Egypt. On seeing the children of Israel encamped in the plains of Moab beyond the Jordan at Jericho as they journeyed, Balak, the king of Moab was filled with fear as he had heard about their victories wherever they passed through and what they had done to the Amorites and to Pharaoh and his chariots. So he sent for Balaam saying: **(Num 22:6) Therefore, I pray you, come now and curse this people for me. For they are too mighty for me. Perhaps I shall prevail so that we may strike them, and so that I may drive them out of the land. For I know that he whom you bless is blessed, and he whom you curse is cursed**. Although he had initially declined, Balaam ended up on the journey. God was angered by this trip so that an angel drew a sword against Balaam. What was God angry about? Simple, He was angry because Balaam was on a trip meant to curse God's Israel. Remember God's vow to Jacob that He would curse whoever cursed him and bless those blessing him? When Balaam finally came to Balak, altars were made in preparation for cursing Israel but every time Balaam opened his mouth, he would find himself blessing instead of cursing Israel to the disappointment of his host. Several times they erected altars in different directions in order to try from every angle to curse Israel. All the time Balaam opened his mouth, he would only bless Israel and not curse. It does not matter which angle your attackers try to come from, your God will stand that corner. Nothing will by any means hurt you. From finance, health, relationships, work, family to ministry or whichever angle the enemy may try to erect his alters against you, he cannot succeed. No weapon formed against you can prosper. You are more than a conqueror through Christ Jesus. So be still and peaceful. Balak was very desperate for this curse to take effect and was angered by Balaam's blessing of Israel. Balaam responded telling him that Israel could not be cursed for God stood in their defence. *(Num 23:7) And he took up his parable, and said, Balak the king of Moab has brought me from Aram, out of the mountains of the east, saying, Come, curse Jacob for me, and come, defy Israel. (Num 23:8) How shall I curse whom God has not cursed? Or how shall I defy whom Jehovah has not defied? (Num 23:11) And Balak said to Balaam, What have you done to me? I took you to curse my enemies, and behold, you have kept on blessing them!*

Clearly, no curse can work against Jacob. God keeps covenant and remains faithful even after many generations. Balaam had power to curse and bless according to the words of Balak but all that power could not work against him who God had blessed, Israel. Despite all the errors committed by the children of Israel in Egypt on their way out, God remains adamant that Israel cannot be cursed. He is not able to repent of His promises. The following are the strongest words of Balaam in this matter. *(Num 23:19) God is not a man that He should lie, neither the son of man that He should repent. Has He said, and shall He not do it? Or has He spoken, and shall He not make it good? (Num 23:20) Behold, I have received word to bless. And He has blessed, and I cannot reverse it.*

Balaam is adamant that Israel cannot be cursed because God has only given word to bless concerning Israel and he emphasizes that he cannot reverse the Lord's word, it's impossible. I like it when Balaam continues to say Jacob has no iniquity. *(Num 23:21) He has not seen iniquity in Jacob, neither has He seen perverseness in Israel. Jehovah his God is with him, and the shout of a king among them*. We know very well that things did not always go very well between God and the children of Israel on this journey. You would not expect them to be declared iniquity free like that but what God is saying is that He will uphold His covenant above all things and circumstances. The big lesson here is that no matter how ever much we think somebody has not done it right, God's covenant cannot be challenged neither can God be influenced by what our enemy says about our perceived mistakes. Where people see iniquity, God says Israel has no iniquity. Who are we to see iniquity where God does not? How could God concentrate on mistakes as if He is not the deliverer? Knowing so, God told them in the land of Egypt that when He would see the blood, they would be safe. *(Exo 12:13) The blood shall be a sign for you, on the houses where you are. And when I see the blood, I will pass over you, and no plague will befall you to destroy you, when I strike the land of Egypt.*

God does not see anything on us. He sees the blood of His son, the blood of the lamb. Yes people see mistakes, inabilities and weaknesses but God sees the blood which is a continuous covering on us. So I say to you my brethren, stay in the blood of the Lord Jesus Christ. Don't move a bit no matter what. If you ever make a mistake, do not delay, repent speedily and keep covenant in place. Remember He says when we confess our sins they will be forgiven without any shred of a doubt as this is God's quality. *(1Jn 1:9) If we confess our sins, He is faithful and just to forgive us our sins and to cleanse us from all unrighteousness.*

All God remembers about Israel is covenant. God defends Israel against every spell or curse. *(Num 23:23) Surely, there is no spell against Jacob, nor any fortune-telling against Israel*. No spell, no curse can be brought upon Jacob. Everything will be turned in Jacob's favour while condemning them who design the curses and spells. We will revisit the story of Balaam and the talking donkey later in this book.

No tongue can rise against Israel and succeed. You must not fear them who talk in dark corners and point fingers at you. No amount of words can turn God against you or persuade Him to change His mind on you. As words mount like a flood against you, you may almost think God has heard enough negative things talked against you and He now thinks like the gossipers. No, He does not need to be told about you. He values His relationship with you and loves you without reference. There are no special people who can claim to be God's advisors on your life. He deals with you as an individual and should you have any issues, God is ever so ready to work them out with you without condemning. God will send you the right people to encourage and help you understand His word but that does not make them advisors to God on your life. You must be able to discern the difference between those with authority to rebuke and teach you and those claiming what they are not. Remember God cannot repent calling you. All those tongues being waged against you can only attract God's anger to themselves. *(Isa 54:17).. And every tongue that shall rise against thee in judgment thou shalt condemn. This is the heritage of the servants of the LORD, and their righteousness is of me, saith the LORD.*

Every tongue that shall rise against you in judgment, you shall have the authority to condemn. Israel cannot be cursed. May be the only way to fight Israel is only dependant on the double coincidence of two things, the time when God wants to punish Israel and that He chooses to use you to do so. This means that you may be able to hurt Israel at a time God may want them to learn a lesson and repent. However, you stand the risk that when Israel has learnt their lesson and repented, they will overcome you and your position will be worse than before as God will then stand with Israel against you and bring complete destruction in your camp. Some nations and kings including the Philistines, Amorites, Nebuchadnezzar and Pharaoh have found themselves in this predicament. Once the children of Israel wept by the rivers of Babylon as they remembered Zion, which was their repentance. The next thing you hear is that Babylon is fallen. *(Jer 51:8) Babylon is suddenly fallen and destroyed.* So the bottom line is that Israel cannot be cursed. If at all God has something to rebuke Jacob on, it will be perilous for us to think that He is inviting us to join in to condemn him. There is no person loved by God who He does not rebuke as He trains them His ways and as they are all human who from time to time need correcting. Even Abraham had a hard time when he lied that Sarah was his sister, letting another man take her to bed, almost sleeping with her had God not intervened. This does not licence us to curse Abraham as we are blessed in him and are not in any way more righteous than him. If God would rebuke Abraham, certainly this would not mean he has been thrown to us for ridicule and abuse. No one can curse Abraham of God, not even Melchizedek who only blessed him. Did Isaac not fall for the same challenge introducing Rebekah as his sister, only to be seen by the King of the Philistines caressing her? *(Gen 26:9) And Abimelech called Isaac and said, Behold! She surely is your wife. And why did you say, She is my sister? And Isaac said to him, Because I said, Lest I die on account of her.*

When Moses smote the rock twice at Meribah, God was angered to the extent of even barring him from entering the Promised Land, telling him he would only see it but never enter due to this error. Scripture shows that God wanted Moses to talk to the rock but due to insults hailed on him by the people he was leading, he grew impatient and instead of talking to the rock, he smote it twice to produce the much needed water. While plenty water gushed out after Moses had smitten the rock twice, this did not go well with God who wanted him to talk to the rock in front of the children of Israel. *(Num 20:8) Take the rod, and gather the assembly, you and Aaron your brother, and speak to the rock before their eyes. And it shall give forth its water, and you shall bring forth to them water out of the rock. So you shall give the congregation and their animals drink. (Num 20:11) And Moses lifted up his hand, and with his rod he struck the rock twice. And the water came out plentifully, and the congregation and their animals drank. (Num 20:12) And the LORD spake unto Moses and Aaron, Because ye believed me not, to sanctify me in the eyes of the children of Israel, therefore ye shall not bring this congregation into the land which I have given them*.

There are many important theological teachings on this particular event but we shall only dwell on our subject. While God had strong words for him and even a judgement, it does not open Moses for us to ridicule, curse or condemn as the same God demonstrated that only Moses could speak with Him face to face like a personal friend. Theirs was a special relationship between the two and no man could interfere. *(Exo 33:11)   And Jehovah would speak to Moses face to face, as a man speaks to his friend.* Even by any comparison, what good work in the Kingdom of God could you have done in order for you to rise above Moses and be able to condemn and curse him? This man was God's choice for about the biggest task ever. He had seen the burning bush and received a mandate from God to lead His people out of Egypt to the Promised Land. Moses was the only person able to ask God His name. He had stood against the Pharaoh, working stunning signs and wonders including seeing God unleashing various curses which tormented the Egyptians.

Moses had presided over a very arrogant and faithless generation of Israel, journeying through the deserts and seeing the Lord release manna and quails for food. He, and him alone, had gone up the mountain to receive the commandments from God, coming down aglow with glory so much that the children of Israel had to ask him to cover his face as they could not look at him due to the glory. He is the one who ordered the red sea to part so the children of Israel could pass, resulting in many Egyptians perishing in the sea as it closed after the Israelites to fulfil Moses' word that they would not see those Egyptians anymore. *(Exo 14:13) For the Egyptians whom you have seen today, you shall never see them anymore*. This day Moses, by his God, overcame the invincible Pharaoh and his chariots which were feared worldwide. What level of miracle did Moses not command? He had chosen to stand by God's people over being a prince in the royal family of Pharaoh.

God does not forget what works were done for Him by any one of us. How in our minds could we ever think God would forget Moses' works? *(Heb 6:10) For God is not unrighteous to forget your work and labor of love which you have shown toward His name, in that you have ministered to the saints, and do minister*. While people do forget whatever is done for them by others, God is not that unrighteous to forget. This explains that it is unrighteousness that makes people forget whatever is done for them by others and even by God. God is not like men.

God cannot forget. You can take that to the bank. There are those amidst us who served the Lord from a young age. Some even gave up any schooling opportunities they had as they felt they needed to move with the gospel, many times going without decent food and clothing while they used the little they ever got, if any, to enhance the work of the Lord and to help others. Things may look dull now as if the same sweet God you served has forgotten all about you. You are just, like, thinking of all missed opportunities and resources spent on some who needed help and now scorn at you in what looks like their success. People who used to see you up the stage singing or praying for people are wondering what happened. You used to sleep in the worst places in the villages and so many came to the Lord, some of whom are pastors and leaders of ministries today and yet it looks like nothing good came your way. The good news is that God is not unrighteous to forget any of your labours. All is safely banked and in the twinkling of an eye, it will not be surprising when the Lord shall lift you up as He will come back for the good work you did. God does not forget. Do not be too hard on yourself, the reward is around the corner. Something big will soon happen and those who thought you had been forgotten will want to stand on your side again. The Lord shall honour you at an unexpected time and give you access to many opportunities and doors others fail daily to break through. Let's go back to Moses.

One incident with the rock cannot define Moses otherwise. There is no child loved by his father and yet is not chastised by him. Do not be fooled, God's love for Moses could not be compromised. To demonstrate His love, when Moses finally died, God held a funeral alone. It was God's loss. God Himself buried his friend,

Moses, in the valley in the land of Moab. *(Deu 34:5)* *And Moses the servant of Jehovah died there in the land of Moab, according to the Word of Jehovah. (Deu 34:6) And He buried him in a valley in the land of Moab, opposite Beth-peor. But no man knows of his grave to this day.*

Do you know anybody else who was buried by God or have you ever been to a funeral where God was physically present helping with the duties there? Only Moses was buried by God who dug and prepared a curve for a tomb and did all that was necessary for burial. God was the grieving relative and next of kin of the late great man. Do you still think you can curse or condemn Moses? I don't think so. There are many men of God whom, due to our ignorance, we think low of and let loose our tongues concerning them. The first question that must come to our minds is whether we have ever done better than them. If you curse Israel, God will himself curse you. God defends Israel even in his absence. Israel may not hear you cursing him but God watches Jacob's back, He will curse you in turn.

If in one or two scriptures we may have heard God shouting at Jacob, it is between God and his man of choice and never for us to misconstrue for Jacob having been thrown to the dogs. God rebukes His beloved. Even Jesus often had strong words for Peter and yet you would only fool yourself to think Peter would be thrown away. Never, they were so close that Jesus left him to feed the flock as He ascended. *(Joh 21:16) He said to him the second time, Simon, son of Jonah, do you love Me? He said to Him, Yes, Lord, You know that I love You. He said to him, Feed My sheep.*

God's name includes the name of Jacob. It is therefore very difficult to mock him without mocking God. God's name is the 'God of Abraham, the God of Isaac and the God of Jacob'. This is what defines who Jacob is. The man in God's name! Even the name Jacob, although changed to Israel during the wrestling, is not hated by God. He refers himself as the God of Jacob and not many times the God of Israel. God likes the name Jacob. It is the name that describes the battles fought to bring this man to the   position of first born where he would otherwise have been second. If God calls himself by that name, who are we then to theorise on it negatively? Jacob is God's favourite name. It must be yours too if you are on God's side.

Jacob, Israel, cannot be cursed. Earlier in this book we discussed the case of Balaam, who, after refusing for a while ended up on a journey to curse Israel at the behest of Balak the king of Moab. I promised we would revisit it. God could not rest once there was a plot to curse Israel. Although Israel may not have been aware of this evil plot against them or even that a special cursing agent had been invited, they were as safe as ever because they enjoyed a protection promise where God was to watch Israel's back and curse all their enemies for them. That is why you must rest peacefully on the promise of protection from the

Lord Jesus Christ. To all who received Him Jesus gave them power to become children of God who enjoy the protection of their father. If God be for us, then who can be against us? We look at the event again, more closely this time; *(Num 22:5) He sent messengers therefore to Balaam the son of Beor, to Pethor, by the river of the land of the sons of his people, to call him, saying, Behold! A people come out from Egypt. Behold! They cover the face of the earth, and they are staying across from me. (Num 22:6) Therefore, I pray you, come now and curse this people for me. For they are too mighty for me. Perhaps I shall prevail so that we may strike them, and so that I may drive them out of the land. For I know that he whom you bless is blessed, and he whom you curse is cursed. (Num 22:27) And when the donkey saw the Angel of the LORD, she lay down under Balaam; so Balaam's anger was aroused, and he struck the donkey with his staff. (Num 22:28) Then the LORD opened the mouth of the donkey, and she said to Balaam, "What have I done to you, that you have struck me these three times?" (Num 22:29) And Balaam said to the donkey, "Because you have abused me. I wish there were a sword in my hand, for now I would kill you!" (Num 22:30) So the donkey said to Balaam, "Am I not your donkey, on which you have ridden, ever since I became yours, to this day? Was I ever disposed to do this to you?" And he said, "No." (Num 22:31) Then the LORD opened Balaam's eyes, and he saw the Angel of the LORD standing in the way with His drawn sword in His hand; and he bowed his head and fell flat on his face*.

God promised to curse whoever curses Israel whose other name is Jacob. We later see Balaam and Balak trying in vain to set altars on different places and angles to curse the children of Israel. In all cases Balaam just found himself blessing instead of cursing this nation. He later on conceded that these particular people were not cursable as God had blessed them. They had a tag of blessing upon them. He asked how they could be cursed when God does not curse them. It was concluded the efforts to curse Israel were futile. The end result was that Balaam, called to curse the children of Israel, ended up blessing them, not once, not twice, but even three times and more to the displeasure of the king of Moab against who the words of Balaam began to prophesy. Balak was extremely angered and rebuked Balaam who insisted Israel could not be cursed and nothing could change that. *(Num 24:10) And Balak's anger was kindled against Balaam, and he smote his hands together: and Balak said unto Balaam, I called thee to curse mine enemies, and, behold, thou hast altogether blessed them these three times*. You are advised to read more in your bible on this issue. It does not matter which angle the enemy stands on, Israel cannot be cursed.

Chapter Eight

The Lord's Annointed

Do you remember how David refused to touch Saul? Although it was Saul seeking David's blood, he still made sure he did not lay his hand against the anointed of the Lord. It was even at a time God had rejected Saul and replaced him with the same David and yet this young prudent man could not take chances knowing how God could just turn around for His anointed. A certain man thought he would appease David by claiming he had killed Saul. David immediately ordered him killed for touching the anointed of God. This man may have died in vain. Saul had deliberately fallen upon his own sword in order to kill himself and not be killed by the sword of his enemy according to scripture and nowhere is it mentioned this man had killed him. *(1Sa 31:4) Then said Saul to his armourbearer, Draw thy sword, and thrust me through therewith; lest these uncircumcised come and thrust me through, and abuse me. But his armourbearer would not; for he was sore afraid. Therefore Saul took his sword, and fell upon it. (1Sa 31:5) And when his armourbearer saw that Saul was dead, he likewise fell upon his sword, and died with him.*

It is clear Saul fell on his sword and died together with

his amour bearer. Who is this man reporting having killed Saul? Why was he doing it? He thought like today's Christians that David would rejoice at the demise of his senior who was supposedly standing in his way. He thought Saul, whose behaviour did not make things any better, was a sinner worth the ridicule. David ordered this man killed for saying he had killed Saul. He died for saying the wrong words. It looks like this man had a misconception that David would be pleased with someone killing Saul who had sought to kill him. But David would not be found standing between God and His anointed, a virtue today's worshipers are bankrupt of, no wonder why many are sick and weak amidst us. *(2Sa 1:14) And David said, Why were you not afraid to stretch forth your hand to destroy Jehovah's anointed? (2Sa 1:15) And David called one of the young men and said, Go near; fall on him. And he struck him so that he died. (2Sa 1:16) And David said to him, Your blood be upon your head, for your mouth has testified against you, saying, I have slain Jehovah's anointed*.

Can you notice that David continued to respect Saul's anointing? Was there ever an incident he talked about Saul falling out with God? How could he ever have spoken like that? Does anyone ever know anything that happens between God and His servants? It does not matter what it looks like, we simply cannot tell. Even when we later visit the same David who God called the man after His own heart, how many errors can we count on him? So many, from ordering a census on Israel to taking Uriah's wife and getting him killed at battle and yet he is God's friend. Had he rejoiced at the death of Saul or ordered it, what would have been his ending? Someone else was going to kill him also. Throwing stones, as what Jesus revealed, is only done by guilt ones trying to appear better when they are not. When Jesus, rescuing the woman found in the so called act, asked those who had never done like her to proceed stoning her, He found as He lifted His head that all had gone without a single stone thrown. *(Joh 8:7) But as they continued to ask Him, He lifted Himself up and said to them, He who is without sin among you, let him cast the first stone at her. (Joh 8:8) And again bending down, He wrote on the ground. (Joh 8:9) And hearing, and being convicted by conscience, they went out one by one, beginning at the oldest, until the last. And Jesus was left alone, and the woman standing in the midst. (Joh 8:10) And bending back up, and seeing no one but the woman, Jesus said to her, Woman, where are the ones who accused you? Did not one give judgment against you? (Joh 8:11) And she said, No one, Lord. And Jesus said to her, Neither do I give judgment. Go, and sin no more.*

Do you think there were no holy people in that land? I am referring to non-adulterers. They simply had not come to throw stones because those better than you do not condemn you, only the worse. Whenever you see someone gossiping about another, that's a sure sign, they are no better. Could you ever imagine all those who had come to stone the woman were adulterers? Yes they were; that's why they all disappeared when the Lord allowed those who were not like the woman to start throwing stones. Only those with weaknesses seek to punish others for what they have not overcome themselves. The righteous did not come to throw stones. They normally pray for others instead of plotting.

Jesus is known as the son of David. Who are we then to want to curse David? Solomon is the son of Bathsheba, the former wife of Uriah. Well, at the end of the day it all remains between God and His anointed. We are safer without interfering. The birth of the Saviour follows the linage of Solomon without the scriptures trying to hide that Solomon is the son of David born of Uriah's former wife. *(Mat 1:1) The book of the genealogy of Jesus Christ, the son of David, the son of Abraham.(Mat 1:6) and Jesse fathered David the king. And David the king fathered Solomon of her who had been wife of Uriah*. All said and done, David remains the man after God's own heart. The plans and purposes of God are so remote to our understanding. It is not like God did not rebuke David, yet He did not disown him. Those who He loves, God rebukes and yet does not give room for the devil to take advantage of His people's failures and weaknesses as that does not benefit God's Kingdom.

Chapter Nine

Chariots of Fire

B ack to Jacob, we have seen how it all happened and how God himself chose and uplifted him. So where did the idea come from that churches preach evil of Jacob whose name is joined to God's? This has come about by generalising biblical stories without understanding the intentions of God Himself. Isn't it just the same thing like the whole world believing that Elijah went to heaven by a chariot of fire when scripture openly tells of him going by a whirlwind? While the scripture is so open, the point of concern is how big preachers all over the world stand on very important platforms to speak about Elijah going to heaven in a chariot of fire contrary to the record of the actual episode in the scriptures. I remember one charismatic preacher describing how God decided to put Jesus as the only way after having seen people 'arriving in heaven anyhow like Elijah in a chariot of fire and God was concerned some may soon arrive on bicycles'. This is one of the most abused scriptural episodes of all time. He did not go by chariot. *(2Ki 2:1) And it happened when Jehovah was to take Elijah up into Heaven by a whirlwind; Elijah went with Elisha from Gilgal. (2Ki 2:11) And it came to pass, as they still went on, and talked, that, behold, there appeared a chariot of fire, and horses of fire, and parted them both asunder; and Elijah went up by a whirlwind into heaven.* This preacher seems not to understand the purpose of the coming of Jesus. He seems to think Jesus came to halt more objects landing in heaven. As if any UFOs ever landed there! It wasn't so. We were dying in our sins as scriptures point that all sinned and fell short of the glory of God. Therefore God gave His only begotten Son to die for us that whosoever would believe in Him would not perish but have everlasting life *(John3:16).* This is not something to play around with. This is the grace of the Father to this would be doomed humanity.

The foregoing shows how much abuse God's scripture has suffered. This is mere lack of knowledge showing us that while we may have eyes, we see not and while we may see, we do not perceive until the Holy Spirit dwells in us. The Spirit of the Lord which creates an honest earnest desire for God's true word is needed upon each and every believer before it can be guaranteed that the teachings that are delivered day in and day out in our churches and on television stations have anything to do with God and His Christ at all. Scriptures must be read for self-nourishment. The book of Psalms calls it meditating upon the law of the Lord. In this instance 'law' stands for 'word.' *(Psa 1:2)* *But his delight is only in the Law of Jehovah; and in His Law he meditates day and night.* We need to spend time on the word, praying and allowing it to work within us. The word is not read for preaching. It can be dangerous to eat food prepared by him who does not partake of it. Preaching should just be a sharing of what is in us, in our hearts as it is written: *(Mat 12:34)...out of the abundance of the heart the mouth speaketh*.

Probably from the days you heard about church, one of the most common stories spoken of was that of Elijah going to heaven in a fire chariot. How much does God wonder when He looks from above and sees the development of error overtaking the teaching of the truth? God would almost want to yell and say 'there is no parking for chariots in here'. How much is He shouting to no avail that we must know the truth which alone will set us free as fiction and religious stories won't? Think about it. Is not this the reason why Jesus taught that if what we call light in us is not light at all then we are in great darkness? *(Mat 6:23) If therefore the light that is in you is darkness, how great is that darkness!* Of course it is darkness to pray quoting that Elijah went to heaven in a chariot of fire and claim it as God's word when it is not. It is darkness to think the word of God says that when it does not and yet day after day the same is someone's most quoted scripture. To him it is light. So if what he calls light is darkness, then how great is that darkness? Claiming from God an experience like that of Elijah and the chariot will only silence Him as none of His word says that and never was there such an occurrence of events. We need to know the truth.

Jesus did never say the truth would set us free. Only the truth that we do know will. *(Jn 8:32) and ye shall know the truth, and the truth shall make you free*. Note how Jesus begins by mentioning knowing before He talks of being set free. We must know the truth before it can affect us. The truth that we do not know cannot free us. This is the simple reason why some are still bound even after two thousand years of the work of the cross. It is simple. They do not know the truth yet. Although the truth is there, it cannot set them free. When they shall know it, they will be set free. Only the truth that we know will set us free. God complains His children perish due to lack of knowledge. In the absence of knowledge there is no freedom, there is no victory. *(Hos 4:6) My people are destroyed for lack of knowledge*. It is the lack of knowledge that leads us to say whatever we think about Jacob, Elijah and many others. May God help us!

Chapter Ten

Jesus: The Rejected Stone

The Americans and the British believe it as governments that they cannot be Israel's enemies. The greatest doubt on whether Barack Obama would be a good American president hinged on his perception of Israel. They feared he may not be a friend to Israel. Those close to him and his foreign policy did a good job convincing voters Obama was pro-Israel. It was such a crucial aspect in the election as the Americans and the British are aware no nation curses Israel and prospers. The Palestinian problem could be solved by both Jews and Palestinians accepting Jesus Christ through whose blood they could be made one people bought and reconciled to God once and for all, enabling them to live together under the new covenant which does not reduce the Jews but enhances them and brings all those bought by the blood under the same Father who sits upon the throne. Denying the existence of Israel does not help matters. There is no solution without accepting the authenticity of Israel. The warring sides spend time and millions of scarce dollars and pounds seeking a solution and yet the acceptance of who Christ is remains the true solution. Jesus Christ is the stone these builders are rejecting no wonder why they construct nothing durable. Rejecting Jesus Christ continues to be the bottle neck in all endeavours and efforts for a solution. How many can successfully build a corner house without the corner stone? They labour in vain who build without the Lord so do those who watch without Him. *(Ps 127:1) Unless the LORD builds the house, those who build it labour in vain. Unless the LORD watches over the city, the watchman stays awake in vain*. Without Jesus as the solution, there will not be a solution until He shall descend to reign. He is the missing link, the stone the builders are ignoring. Peace talks after peace talks yield no substance until the chief corner stone is picked up. Jesus Christ is the head corner stone. *(Mat 21:42) "The stone which the builders rejected, this One has become the head of the corner; this is the Lord's doing, and it is marvellous in our eyes?"*

The word of God must be read with an anointing so that we can understand the simple things meant for our benefit. Like I have mentioned already, it behoves me to mention that only the truth that we know can set us free. Knowledge ought not to be equated to hearsay. Religious stories told from defunct mission houses have often been taken for the word of God. Church stories which found their way in through culture and other influences ended up being accepted by some in place of God's word. The word of God is beyond all that and remains unchanged forever. Heaven and earth may pass away but His word will remain forever established. The word of God is powerful and as such cannot be like any stories coming out of tabloids and other forms of media which are orchestrated by people for varying agendas. The word was there before the beginning and shall be there after the end. *(Mat 24:35) The heaven and the earth shall pass away, but My Words shall not pass away.*

It is simple, God cannot abandon covenant. For this reason the Lord ensured the coming of the Messiah as He was promised to the Jews and also the gentiles. The Lord had a promise already in place that a Saviour was to be born who would help Israel out of their sin. It was through the Saviour that people in great darkness would see the light. Because He cannot forget Israel, God remembered them through a new covenant as a way of salvaging them from the one they had broken. Jeremiah told of a new covenant which would help the sons from the sins of the fathers which had become difficult to overcome and erase. In His love for them God decided to give Israel and all people on earth a new beginning so that no person would blame their background for failure. Each person was to be given a new beginning through a rebirth which is only in Christ Jesus. Once born again, all things would become new, old things having passed away. This is not something announced in the New Testament. God began announcing it in the Old Testament through prophets and priests. God continued to speak of the new things that would come in the days ahead. *(Jer 31:33) but this shall be the covenant that I will make with the house of Israel after those days, says Jehovah: I will put My*

Law in their minds, and write it on their hearts; and I will be their God, and they shall be My people

To the prophet Joel, the Lord promised the pouring of His Spirit upon all flesh which would come to pass in those days to come. It was well announced so much that it is more difficult to deny it than to believe. This time it was all flesh and not only Israel. God had decided to bring all the people on earth, all flesh under the same power of the Holy Spirit to enable them to have the same understanding of the word of God and to become one great family of Him who called all out of darkness. *(Joel 2:28) And it shall come to pass afterward, that I will pour out my spirit upon all flesh; and your sons and your daughters shall prophesy, your old men shall dream dreams, your young men shall see visions: (Joel 2:29) And also upon the servants and upon the handmaids in those days will I pour out my spirit*.

At this time we can see the Lord would not make any distinction between master, slave, servant or hand-maids. That would be a completely different time altogether where gender would not have any place. Male or female, young or old, servant or master all that did not matter. The Lord was going to work with all the willing flesh. As long as you are flesh you really are the one for this one. This is what is brought by the new covenant in Christ Jesus.

Chapter Eleven

Covenant People

D id you know that we are God's covenant people through Christ Jesus who has made us heirs of the father and joint heirs with the Son *(Rom 8:17)*? Like unto Jacob, God has a covenant with all who have believed in His plan of salvation, Jesus Christ His only begotten Son. A covenant for all; it is a covenant that is sealed by the blood of His own Son Jesus Christ and no longer the blood of bulls and lambs. It is a better covenant that speaks better things. It is a covenant which operates through our faith in God and obedience to His word, all through His only begotten Son Jesus Christ. *(Heb 7:22)... by so much was Jesus made a surety of a better covenant.* We are to see greater things than were seen in the old covenant. Jesus Himself promised that we would do greater works once He had gone to the father. *(Jn 14:12) Verily, verily, I say unto you, He that believeth on me, the works that I do shall he do also; and greater works than these shall he do; because I go unto my Father.* Why when He had gone to the father? Because the covenant would have been confirmed by the pouring of His blood at the cross and having performed the priestly work before the father in Heaven! Before this was done, Jesus would be on earth preaching the new covenant and teaching about its coming. Therefore all the miracles were more of a demonstration of what the covenant offered which would open widely when He went to the father. Before then, the lamb had not yet been offered and its blood not yet delivered before the altar. Like Isaac would ask; where was the lamb for sacrifice? Where was the priest to administer the sacrifice? Jesus became all in all as He was everything needed for the ceremony. He was both the lamb and the high priest. The new covenant is the one which, unlike the old, concerns every soul on earth. It is the ultimate covenant as it encompasses all races and classes of people without limiting God's activity to just certain people but is open to all. While the old covenant depicted God moving with a chosen people, the later shows God as the God of every soul. It becomes the better covenant both for us and God. If you believe Him to be the God of the whole universe, you will want to see a covenant like this one. Jews, chosen as they may be, have to show their understanding of their God by moving with Him through the covenants. Imagine if the Israelites had become hard hearted in Egypt and refused to abide by new instructions boasting of their old heritage. They would have landed in the same plagues as the Egyptians themselves or didn't some of them? At a certain time God had to come up with something to differentiate the obedient from the rest. He instructed Moses to preach of the blood. They had to put blood on their door posts. God, at this time would not seek to know the nationality of each individual. He would come against those without the blood and destroy in their families. *(Exo 12:12) For I will pass through the land of Egypt this night, and will smite all the firstborn in the land of Egypt, both man and beast; and against all the gods of Egypt I will execute judgment: I am the LORD*.

God did not say what nationality would suffer the plague but the entire first born generation in the land of Egypt where the children of Israel were also living with their firstborn children. Both Egyptian and Israelite were now the same as they were both in the land of Egypt. The scripture above is   explicit the Lord was that night coming against the firstborn *in the land of EGYPT*. This did not describe Egyptian firstborns neither did it exclude Israelite ones as they both were in the same land. It was now a plague of the land. God would have trusted His people to obey and not perish and would only have been disappointed for those whose households had funerals due to their lack of obedience though they had known Him. At that point God's people would only be spared via their obedience to the provisions put in place from time to time by the Lord. The Lord put in place a way for His people to be saved from the impending distraction. Any household failing to act according to the Lord's instructions would fall victim that night. So the Lord commanded that they would strike blood onto the sides of the door posts of each household. This alone would be the sign that the household should be spared. It did not matter Egyptian or Israelite. If any Egyptian family would do this, they would have their household secured and no firstborn would die. The promise was that anyone under a house with door post sides stricken with blood would be spared. God would pass without inflicting any harm there. Look at this: *(Exo 12:13) And the blood shall be to you for a token upon the houses where ye are: and when I see the blood, I will pass over you, and the plague shall not be upon you to destroy you, when I smite the land of Egypt*. It is important to understand the plague was coming against the land. Why didn't God say when He saw an Israelite then He would pass? This suggests that God was aware there could be some amongst the Egyptians who feared Him while some amongst the children of Israel were rebellious. In demanding to see the blood God would have entered a covenant of emergency with those obeying regardless of nationality. God was offering a way of escape to anyone who believed and obeyed Him. This meant anyone residing there was at risk and only obedience to God's plan for salvation would save the willing. Calming one's family telling them not to worry God was after the Egyptians would breed false hope. Wearing priestly robes and claiming to be God's chosen, the real children of Jacob, would not help. Reciting how Jacob met and wrestled with God all night until he was blessed and got a name change, while so true, would not save any household. There are so many even today who try and choose on what to devote their efforts and avoid obedience. Some prefer to fast where giving is needed with others choosing to pray and ignore fellowship, all to avoid obeying. The result is that we have so many disappointed by lack of results from their efforts. Little do these good people know that God requires obedience more than sacrifice. It is hard to obey. The reason may be that obedience is the major failure of Lucifer. The Lord had been clear, *'And the blood shall be to you for a token upon the houses where ye are'*. Needed was the token and not any rank or race or nationality. God wanted to see the blood for it stood for 'please pass we are in obedience'. As many as did not have the token, the blood on their doors, would have their firstborns killed regardless of some even being Israelite. On the same scale, as many as had blood on the sides of their door posts had their firstborns saved regardless of some even being Egyptian.

If God required the Israelites to obey during those days, what makes anybody think they may just as well continue unheeding the call to come under the blood of Jesus Christ which is today more than a mere token as was the blood in Egypt? The blood of lambs and goats was merely a token while the blood of Jesus is the substance. This is a sign that from time to time people need to respond to God's call for obedience and stop all the theories that God will retract His instructions for one nation. No, God will not do that otherwise His word would not be true. He is not a respecter of persons. *(Act 10:34)... God is no respecter of persons.* He will not see any difference between races and tribes, between nations and tongues, but all are His people created by Him and descending from one man, Adam.

There was time when God chose one nation in order to maintain His will on earth after man had strayed. It was to lead to the birth of the Saviour for the restoration of all. Now He has given power to all who believed in Him to be called the children of God. Not children by nationality or born of the flesh but of the spirit. *(Joh 1:12) But as many as received him, to them gave he power to become the sons of God, even to them that believe on his name: (Joh 1:13) Which were born, not of blood, nor of the will of the flesh, nor of the will of man, but of God.* Like I have often repeated, Jesus cannot be preached as an opinion but the Saviour.

God needs to be glorified by the same nation of Israel taking a lead in believing in God's grace to save and restore all through the power that is in Christ after the failure of the law in the hands of the chosen. While the gentile may not have known God and had not served Him properly in the past, the chosen people knew Him and yet still broke His law leaving both in dire need of redemption hence the coming of the Messiah. God cannot segregate. Now that the grace is offered to all, all will be equal before the just God and can only be separated by their choice to obey or otherwise. *(Rom 10:12) For there is no difference between the Jew and the Greek: for the same Lord over all is rich unto all that call upon him*.

Am I therefore contradicting myself as I say Israel cannot be cursed and yet still declare that they, like all, will need to enter into the newness through

Christ Jesus? No, there is no contradiction. That Israel cannot be cursed demonstrates God's respect for His promises and yet does not exempt the people from obeying today insisting that they once did and trying to salvage the broken law when God has passed that stage, inviting all to the forgiveness in Christ. Speaking through the prophets, God announced clearly that a new and better covenant was coming. In that one, no one would answer for another person. It would emphasize on the individual's relationship with God through His Son Jesus Christ. It would be a relationship lubricated by the Holy Spirit who would empower believers to pray and overcome any obstacles that would come their way.

The father's sins would no longer be transferable to the children who would now be free to exercise their own relationship with the Lord. None of the fathers' errors are to visit them ever. *(Jer 31:29) In those days they shall say no more, The fathers have eaten a sour grape, and the children's teeth are set on edge. (Jer 31:31) Behold, the days come, saith the LORD, that I will make a new covenant with the house of Israel, and with the house of Judah:*

The Lord here announced He would make a new covenant with His people. It was not a covenant for non-Israelite people only as it was made with them in mind and also the gentile. Israel should be quick to accept because they cannot insist on the old one which they did not keep. Even so, God does not seek to punish

Israel for breaking it but to offer them an olive branch by making a new covenant with them, a new one which is unlike the one they broke as it was weakened by the law which offered no power to obey. The new one is strengthened by grace and the power of the Holy Spirit who strengthens us to do the will of the Father and provides continual forgiveness whenever we fail and genuinely repent. *(Jer 31:32) Not according to the covenant that I made with their fathers in the day that I took them by the hand to bring them out of the land of Egypt; which my covenant they brake, although I was an husband unto them, saith the LORD.* The new covenant comes with empowerment to know the Lord so that no person will be forced to obey as the Spirit will be in them. The Lord promises to forgive all sin and give every person an opportunity to start afresh. **(Jer 31:34) And they shall teach no more every man his neighbour, and every man his brother, saying, Know the LORD: for they shall all know me, from the least of them unto the greatest of them, saith the LORD: for I will forgive their iniquity, and I will remember their sin no more.** Ezekiel is also a witness. *(Eze 18:1) The word of the LORD came unto me again, saying, (Eze 18:2) What mean ye that ye use this proverb concerning the land of Israel, saying, The fathers have eaten sour grapes, and the children's teeth are set on edge? (Eze 18:3) As I live, saith the Lord GOD, ye shall not have occasion any more to use this proverb in Israel*.

Can you see that the new covenant abolishes everything that had to do with sin and curses being inherited from the past? Whatever was committed by your father and his fathers cannot be visited on you any longer. God, in this case, actually swears with His own life that it would never be repeated. The sins of the fathers would never be visited upon the children. *(Eze 18:3) As I live, saith the Lord GOD, ye shall not have occasion any more to use this proverb in Israel.* Where God stakes His own life for His promise, we must wake up to the importance of the subject thereof. Past illnesses and suffering should stop as you cross into the blood of Jesus Christ which exonerates you from all blemishes and infirmities of the past with all its ailments, poverty, sin and fear. Nothing of the past shall follow you. Nothing can cross the covenant blood of Jesus Christ following you. All becomes new. You are no longer a carried and brought forward of past generations. In Christ you have an opportunity to be you with your God. The past should not determine your present and future. Not even your personal past should be allowed in as all that has passed away. *(2Co 5:17) Therefore if any man be in Christ, he is a new creature: old things are passed away; behold, all things are become new*.

Only believe and be committed to the walk. You are now in a new covenant where Christ has taken away everything that was designed to put you down. Literally everything, be they ordinances or pronouncements or curses meant to pull you down, Jesus removed. Nothing stands in your way again. *(Col 2:14) Blotting out the handwriting of ordinances that was against us, which was contrary to us, and took it out of the way, nailing*

it to his cross. This is a perfect erasure of the entire negative ever said or written about you. Records may abound evidencing poverty following every member of your family tree descending right to you. It may have been recorded that none of your household ever succeeds in anything meaningful like education, marriage, child bearing, ministry, wealth acquisition, long life or even simple joy. Some of these negative attributes may even be recorded in writing or are public knowledge to the extent you grew up accepting nothing good would ever come out of you. Even your school teacher, knowing your relatives who passed through his class before you, always reminded you that none of your family members ever made it and no hope existed for you no matter how much effort you employed. The word is clear that all of this was taken out of the way and every handwriting of condemnation blotted out. Not only did Jesus take all this out of the way, He also nailed them to His cross. Today, the word of the Lord rebukes every negative saying about you. You will succeed now that the hindrance has been taken away. There is no room for failure, neither is it an option. You are by virtue of covenant designed for success. Do not be deterred by small setbacks which you will always recover from despite negative comments from the vast domain. While loss may come your way here and there, you will always rise to the occasion to the shame of the devil. After every temporary loss or set back you will rise up better, stronger, wiser and readier for bigger and better achievements looking down on the losses as mere battles yet you will always win the war. Remember, battles are not the war. They are mere events in the main war. After all, the Lord will not let you be tempted beyond your ability just like no student is tested beyond what was taught. You are designed to overcome any temptation that may come your way. God will watch over you and make sure He makes a way for you to escape every temptation coming your way. Whenever you encounter any temptation, the correct attitude is to believe it would not come unless God has seen that you can overcome it. *(1Co 10:13) No temptation has taken you but what is common to man; but God is faithful, who will not allow you to be tempted above what you are able, but with the temptation also will make a way to escape, so that you may be able to bear it.*

You will achieve what those before you did not. You are not alone. You are not a loser. The Lord who you are covenanted to is with you throughout. He who called you will never leave you. He will take you the whole way through. *(Phil 1:6) He who has begun a good work in you will perform it until the day of Jesus Christ.* You will certainly succeed. Never look down upon yourself. Do not underestimate what God has made you to be. Nothing shall be impossible to him who believes. With Jesus Christ, all things are possible. You can do anything that you set your mind on and succeed. *(Phil 4:13) I can do all things through Christ who strengthens me*.

You shall not be a subject of ridicule anymore. Regardless of your background, you will rise beyond known limits to a satisfactory life filled with hope and achievement. Those comparing you to your background will soon see that you are a new creation *(2 co5:17)*.

The Lord announces that there shall be no occasion for proverbial mocking of His people as long as He lives. *(Eze 18:3) As I live, saith the Lord GOD, ye shall not have occasion any more to use this proverb in Israel*. It is indeed a better covenant. It is a covenant not of the law but of grace. A covenant not of the letter only but of the Spirit! *(2Co 3:6) … not of the letter, but of the spirit: for the letter killeth, but the spirit giveth life.* You can clearly see how much the father has prepared for us. You can see how much He cares for us. Paul, in the scriptures, is so enthused to announce that God will provide all your needs. He wants us all to know in this new covenant that God will provide according to the economy of Heaven and not your local economy that may suffer recession, depression and credit crunches often characterized by sickening shortages. The Lord will make you different during such times, supplying you according to the economy above. *(Phil 4:19) But my God shall supply all your need according to his riches in glory by Christ Jesus*.

Like many of them have done, the Jews should applaud and accept this covenant and embrace the grace that is in Jesus Christ. Like the scriptures both old and new testaments say, this is a better covenant that speaks of better things. Contrary to popular belief, Jesus did not come to condemn the Jews but to uplift them. In

His sermons, Jesus always uplifted the Jews. Speaking to the woman of Samaria, He declared that salvation was linked to the Jews. *(Joh 4:22) Ye worship that which ye know not: we worship that which we know: for salvation is from the Jews*. This continued to be reflected as Jesus' disciples carried on preaching after His death. We hear Paul putting Jews ahead of the line as he ministered the good news: *(Rom 1:16) For I am not ashamed of the gospel: for it is the power of God unto salvation to everyone that believeth; to the Jew first, and also to the Greek.* Paul had a heart for the Jews to be saved as He insisted they were not to be left out of the new and better covenant. Many Jews accepted this message of salvation and God worked with them. Just as in the land of Egypt when God said *'when I shall see the blood I will pass over you'*, God is still wanting to see the blood. This time it is not the blood of lambs and goats as was the case in Egypt. *(Exo 12:13) And the blood shall be a sign to you upon the houses where you are. And when I see the blood, I will pass over you. And the plague shall not be upon you for a destruction when I smite in the land of Egypt*.

Chapter Twelve

The Blood of Jesus

I t is the blood, the sacrificial blood of God's only begotten Son Jesus Christ. Through this blood we were cleansed and qualified into those to be called God's children. There is something about the blood. It is the meeting place for the Jew and the gentile, the slave and the free, the circumcised and the uncircumcised as well as the rich and the poor. *(Col 3:11)... there is neither Greek nor Jew, circumcision and uncircumcision, foreigner, Scythian, slave or freeman, but Christ is all things in all*.

Jesus' teaching leaves no room for any nation to boast in any way but opens the door for all to enter into the rest through His name alone. We are all now qualified through one standard, the blood. There we are; all who have believed in Jesus Christ are God's covenant people. His protection is upon them who believed. They are no longer under any condemnation. *(Rom 8:1) There is therefore now no condemnation to them that are in Christ Jesus*. Scriptures say you actually become a new creation. *(2Co 5:17)... if anyone is in Christ, that one is a new creature; old things have passed away; behold, all things have become new.* You have become so special to God and are described as royal. He calls you a people for possession. This defines us as a people blessed to possess whatever we lay our choice on. *(1Pe 2:9) But you are a chosen generation, a royal priesthood, a holy nation, a people for possession, so that you might speak of the praises of Him who has called you out of darkness into His marvellous light*;

Those calling upon the name of Jesus have become the apple of God's eye. God will only see the blood of His Son on us and no longer the sinful nature. God will keep watch over these and deliver them from every evil regardless of its origin. Remember Paul and Silas locked up in prison? Just as they began to sing hymns unto God, the heavens responded. They would not be left alone or forsaken. The angels and all the beings in heaven began to engage in a rescue mission. Other prisoners would just listen to the two singing and worshiping their God. But God, who has covenant with all who have come under the blood of His Son was covenant bound to take action. *(Act 16:25) And toward midnight Paul and Silas prayed and praised God in a hymn. And the prisoners listened to them. (Act 16:26) And suddenly there was a great earthquake, so that the foundations of the prison were shaken. And immediately all the doors were opened and all the bonds were loosened*. All they did was to realize that if they did not do something about the situation they could start another day in prison. They did not want to start another day in prison. Their minds were made up and their faith was lifted up to

Him who was able to save them. They decided enough was enough. They remembered the Lord who does not forget covenant. Towards midnight they began to sing hymns unto Him as the scripture says we were called to speak His praises *(1Pe 2:9).* Midnight signifies the beginning of a new day. It was the beginning of a morning. Remember joy comes in the morning. When you have suffered and been bruised, do not give up. Do the right thing: call upon the name of the Lord like these two did. Darkness will soon be overtaken by the morning Jesus brings. *(Ps30:5)* *Weeping may endure for a night, but joy comes in the morning.* At midnight, as they worshiped the Lord, prison gave them up. There was the sound of an earthquake. The foundations of the prison were shaken, casting loose every chain and every prison door flying wide open. The Lord remembered covenant and set them free. The earthquake shook the foundations. I like that. The power that works in us shakes foundations down. The foundations of sin, fear, disease and poverty will soon collapse as you are elevated out of that misery. Just remember to call upon the name of the Lord for there is a promise there. *(Act 2:21)* *And it shall be that everyone who shall call upon the name of the Lord shall be saved."*

Every door flew wide open as the two called. This shows us that closed doors will be open for us as we approach our God in the name of Jesus Christ. All doors regardless of who had closed them will be opened for you if you can only say enough is enough and refuse to start another day in your situation. Refuse to enter a new year in your situation. Do not give up. Even when others do not understand you, do like Paul and Silas who continued to sing to the Lord while other prisoners were just watching. The same prisoners watched them go free. Pain may persist for a night but joy comes in the morning. God was jealously watching over them and in the twinkling of an eye, He delivered them out of prison. You cannot go wrong calling upon the name of The Lord. You cannot sink holding on His name. His name is strong and nothing, I say again nothing can snatch you out of the name of the Lord. You are covenantly safe in there. *(Pro 18:10)* *The name of the LORD is a strong tower: the righteous runneth into it, and is safe*. No death, no disease, no sin, no fear, and no calamity can reach you in there. Every step you take, the Lord will be watching you so that you do not stumble. He does not allow you to lose grip. He will not allow your foot to be moved. Once you take a step, it is secured. You can be ready to take another one. If the enemy and his cheer leaders thought you would lose grip and fall, far from it, you will actually take the next step in whatever you are involved, be it finance, business or ministry. The success of every step you take is guaranteed. Day and night The Lord's eye is on His covenant people. Whatever involves you is guarded by the keeper of Israel who does not sleep or slumber. He will not allow you to lose grip or stumble. *(Ps 121:3)* *He will not allow your foot to be moved; He who keeps you will not slumber. (Ps 121:4) Behold, He who keeps Israel shall neither slumber nor sleep*.

Like He was angry that Balaam was going to curse Israel, God was also angry that Herod planned to kill Peter. God tracked Herod with burning anger on account of His beloved Peter. Like Balaam, Herod, unaware of the Lord's anger over His anointed, continued to address people priding on his intentions to descend on Peter. People were particularly pleased and excited. But God was jealously watching. *(Act 12:6) And when Herod was about to bring him out, the same night Peter was sleeping between two soldiers, bound with two chains. Also guards were keeping the prison before the door. (Act 12:7) And behold! An angel of the Lord stood by, and a light shone in the building. And striking Peter's side, he raised him up, saying, Rise up quickly! And his chains fell off his hands. (Act 12:8) And the angel said to him, Gird yourself and put on your sandals. And he did so. And he says to him, Throw your robe around you and follow me. (Act 12:9) And he went out and followed him. And he did not know that this happening through the angel was true, but thought he saw a vision.*

Unaware the rescue was actually real, Peter continued to think he was seeing a vision. Having gone past the first and second gates and out of the Iron Gate, the angel then departed from him. Peter then realized he was neither dreaming nor seeing a vision. Everything was real. He had been rescued by the angel. *(Act 12:10) When they were past the first and second guard, they came to the Iron Gate that leads to the city, which opened to them of its own accord. And they went out and passed on through one street. And immediately the angel departed from him. (Act 12:11) And having come to himself, Peter said, Now I know surely that the Lord has sent His angel and has delivered me out of the hand of Herod, and from all the expectation of the people of the Jews.*

Peter had been delivered from the hand of Herod and from the expectations of the Jews who were in approval of the King's intentions to kill him. God brought Peter's enemies to shame. He indeed looks after those who have come to Him through Jesus Christ His only begotten Son. From there, Herod did not last one bit more. He had declared himself God's enemy by choosing to be the enemy of God's people. Remember the promise: *(Num 24:9)... Blessed is he who blesses you, and cursed is he who curses you*. At this point Herod is now cursed for plotting Peter's unsuccessful death. For wanting to kill Peter, He will be killed by God instead as God will curse those who curse us. The battle was no longer Peter's. It was now the Lord's. The Lord takes over all our battles. A nation in alliance does not face its battles alone. Its alliance partner will consider itself at war once the other is involved. It is in this sense that the Lord takes over our wars and battles. He maintains our security as His alliance partners. He will declare the battle His and you know what that means. Inevitable victory*! (2Ch 20:15).. Thus saith the LORD unto you, be not afraid nor dismayed by reason of this great multitude; for the battle is not yours, but God's. Herod was soon to die while addressing* *people who, hearing his voice, called him a god. He was stricken dead by the Lord and worms began to eat on his body as if he had died many weeks before. (Act 12:21) And on a certain day, Herod sat on his throne, dressed in royal clothing, and made a speech to them. (Act 12:22) And the people gave a shout, saying, It is the voice of a god and not of a man! (Act 12:23) And immediately the angel of the Lord struck him, because he did not give God the glory. And he was eaten by worms and gave up the spirit*. I hope it is clear to you what kind of action the Lord takes when you are in spiritual or physical trouble. He will not allow you to be harmed. The Lord will curse those who curse you and make sure you always come out the victor in every case. Those blessing you will be blessed. Your situation may seem hopeless like Peter's or like that of Paul and Silas and many who went through even more gloomy situation and yet The Lord will always show up in time to save like He always did, delivering them from imminent danger and death. Likewise He will deliver you from all evil and fill your mouth with laughter.

The scriptures show clearly that ours is a better covenant which speaks better things while all that was done before was a shadow of what was to come. *(Col 2:17) Which are a shadow of things to come; but the body is of Christ*. And yet Jesus Christ is the body of the shadow that was visible from afar. His arrival heralded the reality of what was a dream or a shadow and obviously the body is better than the shadow that is why the new covenant is described as better. It is the body of the shadow confirming we are now in better times under a better covenant. *(Heb 7:22) by so much was Jesus made a surety of a better covenant*. The Lord will defend and protect you till the coming back of His blessed Son.

After Herod had tried in vain to stop Peter and others ministering, it was soon to be found that the word of God actually increased as these gallant disciples fought through all the hardships and continued to trust in their God. There are times when you may think you will never preach this word again due to many hardships that may have come your way. I must encourage and tell you that even Herod could not stop the preaching of God's word. The word actually increased despite the threats as the same disciples did greater than ever while God gave them victory after victory. *(Act 12:24) But the Word of God grew and increased*. I am talking about covenant and how God is sensitive to anything that concerns them who are under covenant with Him in the same way He was concerned about Jacob. Now it is no longer about one nation but about all who received Him. *(John 1:12) But as many as received him, to them gave He power to become the sons of God, even to them that believe on his name*. This is what Jesus was battling to put across to the woman of Samaria who held on to the notion that the Jews were not to eat with the Samaritans and that while these would worship in the mountain the Jews worshiped in Jerusalem. While not ready for the change, she got the shocker as the Lord announced to her that things had changed. It was not about the place of worship anymore; neither was it about Jew nor Samaritan but that it had all gone spiritual. God was to be worshiped in spirit and truth not in the mountain or in Jerusalem. This was a new way of worship that pleased the father. *(John 4:21)   Jesus saith unto her, Woman, believe me, the hour cometh, when ye shall neither in this mountain, nor yet at Jerusalem, worship the Father. (John 4:22) Ye worship ye know not what: we know what we worship: for salvation is of the Jews. (John 4:23) But the hour cometh, and now is, when the true worshippers shall worship the Father in spirit and in truth: for the Father seeketh such to worship him.*

When Jesus said the hour is coming, it was like something still being planned. He meant that it was to start by one's recognition of the Messiah who was at the helm of the new covenant. As the woman listened Jesus would soon declare that it was now the hour, meaning you have met with the new covenant. It was equally difficult for non-Jews to accept the new covenant that was coming. They would always think worshiping God was not easily accessible. Their conception on worshiping was tightly locked on Jew or otherwise, mountain or Jerusalem. Jesus had brought something new and different. He was teaching that the father was seeking people to worship Him in spirit and truth and not in certain places whose importance had until now become the essence of worship. Things had now changed. It was not surprising the woman at the well would argue with that in the same way some Jews still argue about it today. But God is Spirit and shall be worshiped in spirit and truth. Put it this way: He is looking for worshipers who will worship Him in spirit and truth. Time had come for all to understand that God is Spirit and as such sought a spiritual relationship. *(John 4:24) God is a Spirit: and they that worship him must worship him in spirit and in truth.*

Chapter Thirteen

The Soup

Until this day, the story of the red soup that Esau preferred in place of the birthright and gained him the name 'Edom' remains one of the topical issues in the learning of the scriptures. This is a story of values and choices. It is a story of decisions and preferences. It is a story of wisdom and integrity. Indeed it is a story of vision, focus and achievement.

Taking it from the presentation in the passage of scripture, we learn a lot on the need for Christians to aspire to know and understand the value of salvation. How do we value our position in Christ? Do we have the wisdom to really understand who we are before the face of the Lord? As we are heirs of the father, joint heirs with the Son, do we know that we are regarded by God as His own due to the work done on the cross? Can we value our salvation above all things? *(Phil 3:8)* *But no, rather, I also count all things to be loss for the excellency of the knowledge of Christ Jesus my Lord, for whose sake I have suffered the loss of all things, and count them to be dung, so that I may win Christ.*

Paul, having understood the value of the work done

on the cross, the salvation offered to him while he was not worthy, himself having even been involved in persecuting believers, decided nothing of all he had or had achieved was worthy more than the knowledge of Christ, even societal positions. Therefore he openly declares all things dung compared to the excellence of knowing Christ. He goes ahead and declares that nothing is worthy separating us from the love of Christ. Clearly, soup could not be our choice. Paul takes the stance that even death could never separate us from the love of Christ. This is a clear demonstration of the value one places on what he believes. There is no place for soup whatsoever. *(Rom 8:35) Who shall separate us from the love of Christ? Shall tribulation, or distress, or persecution, or famine, or nakedness, or peril, or sword? (Rom 8:36) As it is written, "For Your sake we are killed all the day long. We are counted as sheep of slaughter."(Rom 8:37) But in all these things we more than conquers through Him who loved us.*

This kind of value understanding was the missing link in the life of Esau and so it is in the lives of many today. Where Esau could not stand hunger even for a few hours, Paul is ready to overcome not only hunger but famine, tribulation, distress, nakedness, persecution, or even peril. When you do not know the value of any given thing, you are most likely to abuse it. Abuse in this case refers to abnormal use (abuse). Christ, knowing the value of being the only begotten of the father, knowing the joy that lay before him, endured the death of the cross. For Him, choosing anything else would have been like choosing soup against birthright. *(Heb 12:2)...who for the joy that was set before Him endured the cross, despising the shame, and sat down at the right of the throne of God*. For enduring the cross, its shame and pain, for the time spent in loneliness and isolation, and for not denying the Father even unto death, Jesus Christ was given the greatest name. He was given a name above every name. *(Phil 2:9) Therefore God has highly exalted Him, and has given Him a name which is above every name, (Phil 2:10) that at the name of Jesus every knee should bow, of heavenly ones, and of earthly ones, and of ones under the earth.*

Esau did not value who he was. He played around and joked about being his father's first born son. He despised the important birthright. Esau put his appetite before the most valuable. He shouted and declared that he did not value his birthright as he thought it was not profitable at that moment and he was bound by his own words. *(Gen 25:32) Esau said, "I am about to die; of what use is a birthright to me?"* His desire for soup was so embarrassing that it earned him a nickname. He was named Edom from this day due to his great affinity for the red soup. *(Gen 25:30) And Esau said to Jacob, I beg you, Let me eat of the red, this red soup, for I am faint. Therefore his name was called Edom*. In other words, he was from that day to be known for his insatiable appetite for the red soup. Imagine being affectionately called 'Red Soup'! How many of us have been named after terrible habits? Food for thought! He exposed himself as a man who cared less about the future and more about the present. He was only concerned about that moment and cared less about the consequences. He was short sighted in his heart and did not want to wait for better things to develop, for better things are not always instant but sometimes have to be nurtured. He lacked vision, settling for sightly gain which would disqualify him tomorrow and forever. For vision sees beyond the walls of today while sight is limited to what is within the walls. It also seems Esau took everything lightly thinking that he had time to change things as and when he wished. Esau, the hunter, was the man with the meat. How he is fascinated by mere soup remains a mystery. While it should have been him being asked for meat, surprisingly he is the one desperate for the soup. It was him who had earned a place in his father's heart by feeding game to the old man. How hungry was he to lay everything down for red soup, mere lentil soup? For momentary relief he gave up an everlasting portion.

There are a few important choices that we can make as children of God and derive satisfaction from them. There is need to be guided by our zeal, love and commitment to the Lord Jesus Christ. We can learn from the errors of Esau on how to choose. We do not choose those things that are comfortable where the uncomfortable bring better results.

From basic living pressures, one can learn that the main

reason why we have fewer people coming to glorify the Lord on worship days is simply that they choose to go to work, visit friends, entertain visitors or catch up on house chores on the day of worship. In England many prefer spending time visiting car boot sales which are notorious for opening on Sundays. These sell discarded household items. Those filthy items are being put first and God last. Others are attracted to the raised Sunday shift hourly rate. This has resulted in a huge population of a distressed people lacking total commitment to worshiping God. Many of them reel with fear, lack of satisfaction and discouragement due to lack of Godly fellowship though they try and comfort themselves by declaring that God is everywhere. While there may be some truths in that, it must however be realised that God is not in everyone. Obviously it is not 'everywhere' who is suffering but everyone missing the opportunity to fellowship in the presence of the Lord where His word is taught in a spiritual atmosphere. It is simply a matter of choice. The inability to see the importance of joining others at a meeting to worship God and instead choose to work a few more hours to increase earnings really constitutes bad choice. It is like choosing soup, exchanging it with birthright to avoid afternoon hunger.

Try and look seriously at our obviously stupid choices which we need to correct before we lose it like Esau. Where we choose not to pay our tithes because we think we need to solve some outstanding challenges. We will be choosing soup ahead of birthright and we already have learnt the devastating consequences related to this. How many times have we avoided doing what we must do in the Lord? May the Lord help us! The absence of knowledge in many Christians has made them settle for less than their legitimate share many times. After having had the soup, Esau could not stand anymore as the rightful person for the blessing. Losing his position, Esau was excluded from the records of the covenant. God was never to be called the God of Abraham, Isaac and *Esau* as his name was replaced by that of Jacob where we hear God telling Moses He was The 'God of Abraham, The God of Isaac and The God of *Jacob'* and nowhere will He be called The God of *Esau*. So near and yet so far! For choosing soup, Esau lost God and yet it looked like just a matter of birthright. There are a lot of things that look so simple and not that important and yet their effect goes beyond imagination. Did Esau ever think it would go as far as God being called by Jacob's name instead of his? Think about it.

Put it this way, it was either the soup or the birthright. There are times when we must be very careful what we are putting first. It was like he who would partake of the soup would lose the scoop. How surprised was Jacob to learn that big brother could give it all up just for the soup? As if he was hallucinating, Esau actually said he did not need the birthright which he described as unprofitable in such circumstances. He so much wanted the soup that he spoke ill of his birthright so convincingly that Jacob later on believed him and went for the deal. Esau said the birthright was unprofitable, describing himself as a person nearly dying if soup was denied him. *(Gen 25:32) And Esau said, Behold, I am at the point of dying, and what profit shall this birthright be to me?*

Coward big brother! How could you ever think life depended on soup? If you are not ready to die for your birthright, then what is worth dying for? We know Paul declaring he was not only ready to be bound but to die for the name of the Lord. *(Acts 21:13) .. For I am ready not only to be bound, but also to die at Jerusalem for the name of the Lord Jesus.* But Esau was not ready to suffer hunger for a while and would rather have the soup. It looks like big brother hated anything associated with suffering and pain. If the birthright meant he would go just for the afternoon without the soup, he would rather give it up and have the soup. Esau would not endure the pain of hunger a few more hours. He only needed to wait for the family meal time and his hunger problem would have been solved. He was not ready to wait. We are already noticing a great deficiency of quality, which is imperative as we find a lack of essential attributes in this young man's life. He neither was able to go through suffering nor waiting, yet the two are important virtues desperately needed for the fulfilment of any goals.

Chapter Fourteen

Watch Your Mouth

I t is clear the first born, Esau, had untrained lips. At any littlest challenge, he seemed to say a lot without measuring the power of his words. His negative description of his birthright leaves a lot of questions unanswered for who he was. He had had a recorded close relationship with his father who favoured to eat what Esau would bring above even what his wife could prepare for him*. (Gen 25:28) And Isaac loved Esau, because he did eat of his venison.*

Scriptures show that Jacob did not have as much attention from the father as Esau who was first born. The birthright that had made him the apple of his father's eye is what Esau could publicly denounce. Words are powerful. A young student at Upperview Theological College once said 'words are things'. Whatever you say you are, that you shall be. There are so many people who enjoy calling themselves useless, stupid and poor. Little do these people ever realise that all their words shall come home to roost. Words are things. Words are money. Words are houses. Words are healing. Words are food. Words are prosperity. Words are businesses. Words are weddings. Words are children. Words are victory. Words are miracles. Words can also be much to the contrary; respective to what is being uttered. Some people say very negative words about whatever they have and never take time to thank God for such. They speak ill of their spouses and children. They look down upon their achievements and speak so gloomy of their future.

Some just want to keep on saying they will die any time, lacking the knowledge that by keeping talking about it, they are inviting death. Esau's loose lips got him to forget the importance of the fellowship with his father. Imagine; he was the only one his father called when he was getting ready to die. He may have just spoken in favour of soup and mocked his birthright just as a matter of appeasing other people while he did not think it to be of any consequence. That is why the bible instructs us that our 'no' must be 'no' and our 'yes' must be 'yes'. *(Mat 5:37) Instead, let your word be 'Yes' for 'Yes' and 'No' for 'No.' Anything more than that comes from the evil one."* If Esau had thought it would just end like that, he fooled himself. The mouth is not a joking organ but a creating one, seeing that only through words did God create the heaven and the earth and the fullness thereof.

Remember what is bound on earth is also bound in Heaven. *(Mat 18:18) Verily I say unto you, Whatsoever ye shall bind on earth shall be bound in heaven: and whatsoever ye shall loose on earth shall be loosed in heaven*. It is not like their mother took them back into the womb and rearranged them, no. Those words did the work. The twins were rearranged into a new birth order by the words of the elder which were agreed to by the younger and thus it got bound on earth and heaven had to honour it. Mere words rearranged them from the time Esau spoke against his birthright, renouncing it and proclaiming his younger brother, Jacob, as first born, swearing in the process. It was Esau's offer followed by Jacob's acceptance. Even an ordinary agreement of sale would have been legally completed as it only requires an offer followed by the acceptance (Offer and Acceptance). Everything changed.

Due to the foregoing, the covering had fallen; his secrets with his father began to come open as the mother overheard a plan by Isaac to bless Esau. After all, it was in order for her to discover the plan as Rebekah was a woman on a God mission to make sure the true first born son was blessed. Jacob was the current one after the brother sold his right. The mother, besides maternity notes from local midwives, also had another set of notes about the boys. This was from God. These notes would guide her in how to look after the twin brothers and to make sure the will and purpose of God was fulfilled. Remember, Rebekah was originally barren and Isaac had to pray to God for her to conceive*. (Gen 25:21) And Isaac prayed to the LORD for his wife, because she was barren. And the LORD granted his prayer, and Rebekah his wife conceived*. You can see that this woman was not just one of the many female people having sons or mere twins. She only came to the scene through prayer after having been barren. She was there to fulfil a God appointed mission. She maintained herself within the plan of the Lord by going to ask God what was happening inside her. She sought to understand the mysteries of Him who had opened her womb to conceive, the Lord God. She did not go asking local women and others who profess to know everything. She kept in touch with the Lord. She was swift to hear and slow to speak.

We all need to watch our mouths, guide our lips and tame our tongues knowing the power of this force can be lethal. Whatever you say does not end there. You are what you say. The words you say do not die in the air or disappear with the noises of the traffic. They do not cleave to the ozone layer. Those words are not washed away by the storm. Words are living once said. Everyone will one day meet with their own words in the process of life. You will actually become a product of your confessions somehow. You need to watch your mouth with active vigilance. Train yourself not to say what you are not ready to speak. Rather be a slow talker than allow your mouth to make declarations of what you have not carefully considered, knowing that said words cannot easily be unsaid*. (Jas 1:19) Wherefore, my beloved brethren, let every man be swift to hear, slow to speak*. Consider every word and see if you would repeat it without regret before you say it.

Consider your mouth as a gun and the words as bullets. What can you imagine about this comparison? Imagine all those who hold guns, as many as they are, if they did not take time to consider before pulling the trigger and just shot anyway, anyhow! Try and picture the result and compare the same with those with guns called mouths where we know that it is a gun that everyone holds unlike the metal guns which of cause not every person has access to. The foregoing being the case as it actually is, which type of gun is more dangerous or most likely to be abused? It is obviously the mouth. If you learn to see your mouth as a gun, then you can surely know that there is need for training before use. If you ever discouraged someone from worshiping the Lord or from going to church even if you disliked the pastor or someone in that church, you shot that person down. You shot them with your gun, the mouth and the bullets which are your words hit them. You need to repent.

If you stopped someone by your discouraging words from contributing financially or otherwise to the work of the Lord at any church which calls upon the name of the Lord Jesus Christ, you shot that person with your mouth gun. Those bullets, your words killed him. There are those who begin by saying they do not like talking bad things or gossip when they are actually saying the opposite. They have become accomplished killers. We need to repent on these things. If you hear someone beginning to say they do not like to talk bad or gossip then just remind them to shut up because that's how not to.

How many people lie slain by words? There are so many who could have been great people in the Kingdom of God but threw it all away because somebody shot them down with words. Those who could sing for the Lord were told how bad their voices were or that they were just showing off. Those who could give their money to enhance the work of the Lord were told they were not the only ones, there were others who must also do, they were being taken advantage of, or they were showing off or whatever discouraging words they were told. They were shot down. Be careful who you listen to lest it may be those wanting to hinder you from going to possess the land. They want to shoot you down. God help us, we must not shoot others down. Caleb was not like that. He raised them up those shot down by words and stilled them and told them it was possible.

Let's take another moment of imagination, visualising in our thoughts what it may mean to have a fully loaded AK47 rifle in the hands of someone not trained to use it and yet so anxious to. I think you are already struggling counting the potential corpses in your mind. There are indeed many corpses caused by many untrained mouth users. It is common knowledge that an untrained gun user is a danger not only to the public but also to themselves. This is to say there are many and many who have hurt themselves with their own words worse than they have been hurt by the words of others. Train your mouth through confessing the word of God. Many speak ill of themselves and wake up with a heavy feeling of discouragement every morning. This actually commits the whole day to misery and failure. What good can come out of this? David woke up differently. He would say: *(Ps 118:24) This is the day which Jehovah has made; we will rejoice and be glad in it.*

Where trusted people sent to search out the land of Canaan on behalf of the whole nation of Israel came back and reported describing themselves as grasshoppers   compared to the people of the nation they were spying on, which nation they were supposed to defeat with God on their side, one can only conclude that those words were bullets fired by untrained gunmen. Why bullets? Because the words shot down many who were ready to go and possess the land, but not before they had shot down those saying them who by now should have been feeling grasshopperly. *(Num 13:31) But the men that went up with him said, We be not able to go up against the people; for they are stronger than we.(Num 13:32) And they brought up an evil report of the land which they had searched unto the children of Israel, saying, The land, through which we have gone to search it, is a land that eateth up the inhabitants thereof; and all the people that we saw in it are men of a great stature.(Num 13:33) And there we saw the giants, the sons of Anak, which come of the giants: and we were in our own sight as grasshoppers, and so we were in their sight*.

Let's allow a question time and ask them, 'who says

you are grasshoppers? Did the people of that country call you grasshoppers? Who made you grasshoppers?' The true answer from them should be, 'we did'. It's like asking, 'who shot you down?' when a reckless rifle holder has shot himself on the knee and is now wailing on the ground. They reported for everyone on the same trip without seeking consent. That is what happens many times. Those who talk too much vanity always want to create an impression that everyone is feeling the same. Those disgruntled at church want it thought that everyone is in the same boat. No. We are not in the same boat. We are marching on like South African singer and producer, Itani Madima sang: *'The church is marching on, nothing can stop her now'*.

Learn to speak words of victory. As you speak, believe and it will be so. Caleb had to stand for himself. Saying the opposite of the report of many, he said what he believed. He spoke of victory while others spoke of failure. He spoke of Israel as a victor where others spoke of a victim. What you speak yourself to be is what you become. *(Num 13:30) And Caleb stilled the people before Moses, and said, Let us go up at once, and possess it; for we are well able to overcome it*. Caleb stilled the people. He made them confident. Words can do wonders if they are well applied. The same people who had been exposed to fear by those travelling with Caleb have now heard words of victory, positive words, words that unbundled them from the grasshoppers they had been turned into by negative reporters.

We need to really notice how dangerous these mouth users or gun holders were. They could speak for the Amalekites, the Hittites, the Jebusites and the Amorites who never told them they were like grasshoppers or anything inferior as these were actually afraid of the Israelites and their God and trembling with fear. They actually reported having seen the land and that it flowed milk and honey and yet confessed that they regretted that the men there were stronger than them. Did they find the land flowing milk and honey? Yes they did. Who had first told them the land flowed milk and honey in the first place? God had told them before leaving Egypt that He was taking them to Canaan, the land that flowed milk and honey. *(Exo 3:8) And I am come down to deliver them out of the hand of the Egyptians, and to bring them up out of that land unto a good land and a large, unto a land flowing with milk and honey; unto the place of the Canaanites, and the Hittites, and the Amorites, and the Perizzites, and the Hivites, and the Jebusites*.

That they saw the fruit of the land should have been the greatest boost of their faith. To have proved how precise the word of the Lord had been as spoken by Him should have guaranteed them that they were not alone and that the Lord who had come true in His words about the fruit of the land would be true again in giving them that land. These negative reporters, like newspaper writers, sounded like they knew what was going on when to the contrary, they had their facts upside down. Caleb turned the facts upside up, telling everyone that it was possible. Negative reporters told of the Hittite, the Amorites and others who they called giants, forgetting about their God who had worked mighty visible wonders to get them where they were. They had time to mention the enemy they were afraid of, forgetting God who the same enemy was afraid of.

Caleb said it was possible. He said they would take the land, they were well able. Not only were they able, but well able. The report of one person speaking with authority, confidence and faith overturned the negative by many. It does not take a multitude for victory to come. It takes even just one person standing upon the promises of God and confessing them with his own mouth. In my book Hello Jonah, I wrote, 'One man with God is majority'. Caleb spoke courage into Israel and because of his words people were strengthened to take the journey towards possessing the land. The Lord acknowledged Caleb's faith and fearlessness. His words gave glory to God. He never spoke of failing but winning. His trust in God made a mark and God swore that Caleb would enter the land and possess it even unto his descendants. *(Num 14:24) But my servant Caleb, because he has a different spirit and has followed me fully, I will bring into the land into which he went, and his descendants shall possess it.*

Chapter Fifteen

Be Different

The Lord said Caleb had a different spirit. *(Num 14:24) But my servant Caleb, because he has a different spirit and has followed me fully, I will bring into the land into which he went, and his descendants shall possess it.* There are times when someone should be able to see differently and not always go by public opinion. Can you be different where others speak evil, fear and doubt? Where others opt for the soup, can you be different and go for the birthright? Where others have grown impatient and want to quit ministry can you be different? Where there is gossip, hate and suspicion, can you be different and sow the seeds of love? Be different and be the one to give hope where others faint. Caleb had a different spirit according to The Lord. This actually describes inner intentions. The mouth only speaks from what is full in the heart, says the scripture. *(Mat 12:34)...How can you, being evil, speak good things? For out of the abundance of the heart the mouth speaks.* He was different starting from his inside right to the outside. There are those who want to project a different personality outside when their hearts are heavy with evil intentions. Caleb was not like that. His thoughts, intentions, actions and his words were purely driven from inner commitment. Caleb had a different spirit. What spirit would you say is in you? Why was Caleb different?

Who was he different from? He was different from those who brought a false report simply to discourage the congregation and create a reason for people to want to go back to Egypt. *(Num 13:32) So they spread a false report among the Israelites about the land they had explored. They said, "That land doesn't even produce enough to feed the people who live there. Everyone we saw was very tall, (Num 13:33) and we even saw giants there, the descendants of Anak. We felt as small as grasshoppers, and that is how we must have looked to them."*

They spoke of giants, and other mythical beings in the land. They were lying to create confusion. When the land was finally crossed into, no such giants were found in it. Caleb was able to report as it was. He had not seen anything negative. He had seen what God had promised, the land flowing with milk and honey. Can you compare the two statements and see how determined some people were to mislead the congregation. *(Num 13:32) So they spread a false report among the Israelites about the land they had explored. They said, "That land doesn't even produce enough to feed the people who live there. Everyone we saw was very tall*. I love the King James Version which actually says: '...it is a land that eateth up its

inhabitants.' A false report indeed and so different from the official one and beefed up to discourage the congregation! To Moses, the statement had been different as it was spoken in the presence of Caleb and Joshua who had also gone to search the land and only supported the truth. Look at how it differs, *(Num 13:27) And they told him and said, We came to the land where you sent us, and surely it flows with milk and honey. And this is the fruit of it.*

About the same land, we hear how rich and fertile it is in the official report and yet the congregation is hearing something different. They are being made to think the land is very bad and unfertile and that it would not sustain them. They went that far, to lie about the land from which they even had brought fruit as a sign of its fertility simply to discourage people. In lying to the people they did not know that they were also making God seem to be a liar as He had told them the land was large and rich while still in Egypt. There are many things spoken ignorant of how they tarnish God to whose anger many have fallen victim. *(Num 13:26) They reported what they had seen and showed them the fruit they had brought.*

They had brought proof that the land was good but changed the story completely when speaking to the people just to cause disgruntlement, doubt, fear and discouragement. But Caleb, amidst an unbelieving people who were almost turning back to Egypt despite the distance covered and the time spent towards the

Promised Land, stood his ground confirming that what God had said about the land is what he actually had seen. He stood for the truth. There are those who will go to any lengths to create chaos and discourage the willing. There are so many liars and those who can deliberately misrepresent facts to cause confusion. The devil is the father of lies, seeing that he lied from the beginning. *(Joh 8:44) Ye are of your father the devil, and the lusts of your father ye will do. He was a murderer from the beginning, and abode not in the truth, because there is no truth in him. When he speaketh a lie, he speaketh of his own: for he is a liar, and the father of it.* You cannot be one of them. You need to be different. Supporting a lie puts you in the category where the devil belongs. Did you understand he is the father or the founder of lies? Lying qualifies you as the devil's child. You are God's child. God is the father of truth. Lying only achieves evil. It may sound as if you are being clever, yet you will soon see that it is not profitable. You do not want to be that person always responsible for disrupting God's plan. Refuse to be the architect of the breakdown of ministries.

They were ready to appoint a leader to help them backslide. Every move needs a leader, even backsliding. I am imagining an advert for a leader for backsliding; 'Is there someone amidst all of you who can help us backslide. Someone with strong convictions to rebel against God's plan and His anointed is needed to take us off the vision or even back to Egypt.' This would be an advert you may think would completely have no takers at all. But, alas! You will be surprised how many will respond. If it were not so, there would be no rebellion in the Kingdom of God. All the trusted people, even those who would have been following and standing with the men of God would have continued the good work. But you will still be shocked day in and day out when you learn how many go into gossip, hate and conspiracy against what is clearly God's appointed work. The noises that are made and the negative strength of resistance will tell you there are some leaders making it happen. Let's hear the children of Israel again; *(Num 14:4) And they said to one another, "Let us choose a leader and go back to Egypt."*

You need to be careful when people want to acknowledge you as their person who would be 'able to change things around here.' What do they want you to change which they do not want to follow? Are you really sure you are in the right? Have you considered God's view? Are you not going to rebel against God thinking you are rebelling against man? They thought they were rebelling against Moses and Aaron. They did not have an idea that there was no change needed. It was only them who needed to change their attitudes so that the vision could continue undisrupted. *(Num 14:2) And all the people of Israel grumbled against Moses and Aaron. The whole congregation said to them, "Would that we had died in the land of Egypt! Or would that we had died in this wilderness!*

After this intention to rebel, let us see who was

angered. *(Num 14:11) And the LORD said to Moses, "How long will this people despise me? And how long will they not believe in me, in spite of all the signs that I have done among them? (Num 14:12) I will strike them with the pestilence and disinherit them, and I will make of you a nation greater and mightier than they."* Is it not clear that, contrary to these people's misdirected belief that they were rebelling against Moses and Aaron who they incorrectly perceived as the founders of the journey, they were actually fighting against God? However, the love and tolerance of the leaders is unbelievably great. It was the same leaders, Moses and Aaron who sought the Lord's forgiveness for the rebellious when they could simply have taken it as good riddance. Moses' plea for forgiveness on behalf of them who were rising against him was heard by the Lord who agreed to pardon them. *(Num 14:20) Then the LORD said, "I have pardoned, according to your word"*. I like it when the Lord said He was actually doing this according to Moses' word. It is so clear that God forgave for Moses' sake. It is not the people you see who you plan to rebel against, but God, the same God who appointed them. These plotters risked severe punishment from God and being disinherited according to **Numbers 14:12.** Not only that, the Lord God would have replaced them completely with *a nation greater and mightier than they*. Did I know that these people were not indispensable? Am I reading correctly that God was almost ready to dispense of them and replace them with a greater and mightier nation? This shows that they were not the mightiest on earth. They were only mighty because their enemies feared their God. Actually God is the Almighty. Their might was in their Almighty God without whom they were nothing. I am learning something new here. God could have replaced Israel with another nation anytime. Did you ever imagine that before? I didn't. When we think we are indispensable, we fail to acknowledge the favour of God upon our lives. We delude ourselves thinking we deserve anything when all is simply by His grace and favour. There are those who are beguiled by what they perceive they alone can do in the work of the Lord. They believe no other can do what they do. When they can preach and teach so well, when they can sing and play musical instruments so smooth and operate all technical equipment to the amusement of many, they end up believing things are moving because of them and they actually hold at ransom the whole congregation including the leadership whenever they wish. Little do they know that they are only useful to the extent God appoints them. God could replace them at any time and even disinherit them of those abilities. It does not matter how good one can operate or play an instrument, there is no substitute for discipline and obedience.

When God's favour is withdrawn, nobody will want to listen no matter how skilful one may play. A world renowned powerful pianist only accepted vulnerability after losing important fingers in a boating accident. Do not wait until it happens to you. Learn from the children of Israel and repent and God will strengthen and lift you up.

It's hard to be humble when you are prospering. While winning the war to drive *Mobuto Sese Seko* out of power in the Democratic Republic of the Congo (DRC), *Laurent Kabila* refused an appeal from President *Robert Mugabe* of Zimbabwe and other African leaders to accept a transitional government leading to an election so that he could rule as a democratically elected president. He answered that he would not attend any such talks but only talks on what date the dictator would step down for him. To this, *Robert Mugabe* replied and said it's easy to say anything when one is winning the war but the aftermath was always different. We know how short Kabila's reign lasted and how desperate he was for the support of the international community who could not recognize him as he was not elected. That is why Mugabe, who himself had only taken reign not violently but by an election at independence, had advised him to start out by going through an election process but he refused. Instead of becoming a solution for the woes of his country he ended up as a big part of the problem. My point is to show you that it is hard to be humble in the presence of success and prosperity. This is one of the reasons why some have had to suffer first in order to obey God. Many will only learn when everything is lost and they do not know how to recover. Why wait until all is lost and you are left without any confidence to start again? Why not learn while the flowers still bloom? Never expose yourself to the risk of being disinherited or replaced due to your doubt, ignorance or pride.

As for Caleb who continued urging people to be positive and not to rebel, there was a reward. Let's see again how he stood for the side of The Lord. *(Num 14:9)* *"Only do not rebel against the LORD*." He advised the congregation not to rebel against The Lord. He knew that rebelling against Moses and his leadership meant rebelling against The Lord. He knew what it meant and the losses that would be associated with such a rebellion. They would fail to see the Promised Land with its milk and honey. No one in rebellion would ever see the Promised Land. *(Num 14:21)   But truly, as I live, and as all the earth shall be filled with the glory of the LORD, (Num 14:22) none of the men who have seen my glory and my signs that I did in Egypt and in the wilderness, and yet have put me to the test these ten times and have not obeyed my voice, (Num 14:23) shall see the land that I swore to give to their fathers. And none of those who despised me shall see it*.

When you feel you do not understand anything, rather ask and seek guidance instead of rebelling. After all what you have seen God doing, where are you going? You must never take that attitude that you can also lead like they are leading. That competition does not exist in the Kingdom of God and there is no reward for it. Quite a number of people have started what they think are ministries out of anger, rebellion and competition. We all know that this is not the substitute for God's calling as there is no substitute for it at all. If you think God called you, then where would anger, spite, rebellion and competition come from? The foregoing feelings confirm that you are supposed to be part of the work but you lack the good spirit to follow and obey. There is power in obeying and the rewards come direct from God. So did The Lord ever notice the difference between the obedient and the rebellious or was it for the leadership to notice? At times the leadership may not notice those efforts. It could be the reason why you are hurt. You need not feel that way because we find God really acknowledging Caleb's efforts and rewarding him for that. The reward would benefit generations. Look at this scripture again. *(Num 14:24) But my servant Caleb, because he has a different spirit and has followed me fully, I will bring into the land into which he went, and his descendants shall possess it.* I want you to know that The Lord notices your efforts and they will not go unrewarded. Obedience is always the correct ingredient if you want to have joy while you do the work of The Lord. Some do not wish to obey, preferring to fast even days and nights thinking God will be manipulated by their hunger. No. That could easily present itself as a hunger strike. Learn what is required of you and obey. Humble yourself and accept those put above you by The Lord. Be taught and accept to learn. Learn to serve without wishing to be served. Assume not that you are so special that your absence will halt the work of The Lord. Rather thank God for the opportunity to serve. Simply learn to do the simple. The Lord prefers obedience to sacrifice. *(1Sa 15:22) ... Behold, to obey is better than sacrifice, and to listen*

than the fat of rams.

Disobedience, fear and doubt caused those sent to come back with negative news. They spoke their fear and were so convinced to the extent of persuading the whole congregation to abandon mission. If you speak so negatively like some of those people, you will never possess anything in your entire life. You will talk of the recession, the credit crunch and the falling currency. You will concentrate on how to be defeated instead of putting your efforts on taking your victory which is already guaranteed by Him who began the good work and is faithful to bring it to completion*. (Phil 1:6)* ***Being confident of this very thing, that he which hath begun a good work in you will perform it until the day of Jesus Christ;.***

What you say is very important. What you say comes to pass. In circular language they say what you say is what you get. What you say is the nearest assumption of who you are or can be. So what do you say? Never say what the devil wants to hear. Saying the negative is surrendering when victory was on your side. The devil wants you to say those negative things. So don't say them. Confessing the negative means you signing your rights to the devil. How can you fight and surrender at the same time? Do one thing. **Fight the good fight of faith (1Ti 6:12).** Remain focused on God's promises through His Son Jesus Christ. Only confess to your salvation and victory and you will overcome the world. What you confess is very important. For this reason, salvation is not only by believing, but also by confession. *(Rom 10:9) Because if you confess the Lord Jesus, and believe in your heart that God has raised Him from the dead, you shall be saved*. You must learn to confess the word of God. The power is on your tongue. We must not sharpen skills of complaining and talking of what we think the devil has done, but what we are doing through Jesus Christ. We must not be ashamed to declare all things possible.   It is always the easier thing to say what others are saying and complain together with the rest. It has never been easy to stand out and challenge those you are at par with and stand for the truth. If you do, then you stand the risk of being branded a sell out by those who believe in being on the opposing side always. You may have noticed that there are always those in the work of The Lord who behave like they are an opposition party in parliament. You know that opposition political parties are full time opposers of what goes on. There is no day they are expected to stand up and compliment the government even after building a hospital. They oppose the vision of any government just for opposing. Actually, they legitimately exist to oppose. It does not matter whether in the USA, Britain or Africa, opposition parties are there to oppose. They are actually called opposition parties. Not supportive but opposition! So they do their work when they oppose. Archbishop E. H. Guti once said, 'leave the devil to do his work, you do yours'. During the great recession which hit the world at the time when Obama was taking over the reign in America and Gordon Brown was facing encroaching elections, you could actually see the opposition parties in both countries openly taking advantage of the bad economic down turn to twist public opinion to their advantage. At a time you would think they would stand together to fight one common world enemy, the recession, they actually rode on the bad times to gain political ground. It should not be like that in the Kingdom of God. You must refuse to be an opposing party. Refuse to be the accuser as that is already someone's job description. *(Rev 12:10)... For the accuser of our brothers is cast down, who accused them before our God day and night.* Leave the devil to opposition and do the work of The Lord. The devil is the accuser of the brethren. It is his permanent work not yours. Once you start accusing and opposing the brethren, you have just accepted partnership with the devil. So many people find themselves in this position unaware of the real implications. Refuse being made a false hero by being pushed on to the forefront to oppose what is being done for The Lord. Remember, Caleb refused to join them who planned against the journey initiated by The Lord. It sounded a good plan to make Moses halt the journey and allow people to go back to Egypt. Many supported it with very serious convictions. They thought they were doing it because they were concerned about their children and wives. There is always a way of justifying the wrong that is being done. If you find yourself trying to justify your actions, you are not the only one. It began a long time ago. Let's hear them justifying their rebellion by showing that they are doing it for their children and wives. It started with a carefully planned negative report which could help give the rest a reason to go back to Egypt. The report spoke of a land that eats its people and giants in whose sight the rest of them were like grasshoppers. What some naked lie, simply brought up to cause people to want to go back, to backslide into Egypt. *(Num 14:3) And why has Jehovah brought us into this land to fall by the sword, so that our wives and our sons should be a prey? Would it not be better for us to return to Egypt?* But Caleb stood on the side of the Kingdom of The Lord and refused to join the popular side of those plotting returning to Egypt. Caleb had reached the point of no return which must be the status of every true believer. He never wasted time to say this or that but told the correct story, assuring everyone that it could be done and that they were well able to overcome. He continued to say it was possible. He did not succumb to the voices of the majority. He was the majority. Remember, one man with God is majority. He said, 'yes we can'. His words erased the entire negative that had been said about going into the Promised Land. Imagine, the land was promised, not by man but by God. Your words must be those that erase the entire negative once said about you and your family, about your church, about your pastor and about every God fearing person you know. Your words must be those that will drill a way for you to prosper where none of your family members ever made it. Your words must be those that will cause your church to grow and fulfil its mandate. They must never be your words that will tear apart, distort and delay the work of The Lord in your church. Never shall they be your words that will discourage and demean the pastor and those in leadership. You shall always say 'we are well able'.

The battle of possessing Canaan was won when Caleb addressed the people. He spoke them into confidence, victory and possession. What followed later were simply the results of victory already spoken. Victory spoken is victory attained. 'We can do it, we are well able,' were his words. Let yours be heard.

Chapter Sixteen

No Respecter of Persons

Barack Obama, an American presidential hopeful, taught His supporters to keep on saying 'Yes We Can'. He went on to win the election, making him America's first black president in history. He learnt from a young age to say the positive and to believe he could become whatever he wanted against all odds, even being born to a black Kenyan father and having once attended school in Muslim Indonesia. While millions of black kids were talking negative, adopting gangster names, blaming slavery and confessing perpetual failure and hate, while most of them openly accepted there would never be a black leader in the United States, come rain, come sunshine, Barack Obama needed no gangster name to boost his identity. He believed in God who saw all people equal before Him. He confessed his presidential wishes and read books of positive people like the slain 16th American president, Abraham Lincoln, and learnt to speak positively like them. He spoke and outlined his vision boldly and clearly. He read about and discussed presidents. He did not see or speak of himself as a black inferior ordinary man undeserving of the highest office in the world. He saw himself as God saw him, equal. *(Gal*

3:28) There cannot be Jew nor Greek, there is neither bond nor free, there is no male nor female; for you are all one in Christ Jesus. Barack believed and said he could address the Democratic Party Convention. He never thought there was anything he could not do but believed he could do anything. *(Phil 4:13) I can do all things through Christ who strengthens me.*

Taking one sure step at a time, Barack believed and said he could successfully contest the party primaries. He did not only believe, he said it. Jesus Christ taught to believe and say. *(Mark 11:23) For truly I say to you that whoever shall say to this mountain, Be moved and be cast into the sea, and shall not doubt in his heart, but shall believe that what he said shall occur, he shall have whatever he said.* Can you see that Jesus starts by mentioning the saying part before He talks about the believing part? That is how important words are. It isn't just about believing. Silent faith can end up in the grave without results. Believing and confessing will be the recipe for having it. God spoke creation into existence. Whatever He spoke is what came, not anything else. What He said is what showed up. When He mentioned the sun, it's not the rivers that came but the sun. What you say is what you get. As His children, we can also command things into existence in Jesus' name.

Competing against a more popular, more politically powerful and smart former first lady, Hillary Clinton, who was too established to lose, Barack Obama, married to a black woman, Mitchell, continued to believe and say that he would win the battle, which he did, not so easily though. His most powerful tool is recorded as his sniper speeches which never missed target. He spoke hope. He promised what he had not yet seen himself but only believed. From the onset, he spoke like a president and began to walk like one. Not even mentioning the colour of his own skin, he continued to do what is expected of a nominated candidate and got ready to face the more experienced hero of war, John McCain, who tried in vain to use many tricks in and out of the book to discredit his opponent by calling him a Muslim, 'a friend of terrorists', not a 'real American' and even, a 'socialist' bent on wanting to distribute 'your' hard earned wealth to 'lazy folks'.

It is interesting that there were some blacks who thought he was mad to ever think presidential. After a tougher fight than the party primaries, Obama won with one of the widest margins in American presidential election history, with more whites voting for him than those who voted for former popular presidents like J F Kennedy and Bill Clinton. He became the 44th American president and the first ever black one. He had stood against the whole world of wild media with one weapon, positive words. His speeches were so contagiously full of hope that the whole world wanted to identify with this black presidential candidate. European leaders competed in the race to be the first to congratulate him on his success. While Gordon Brown won the first telephonic conversation, it was his predecessor, now Middle East envoy, Tony Blair, who grabbed the first visit and was described as a friend by Barack Obama. British Prime Minister, Gordon Brown and the opposition leader, David Cameron competed in quoting Obama in their speeches at conferences and even parliament. Barack spoke himself into presidency. What will you speak yourself into? The important thing is that he learnt to confess it even when it looked impossible. Without being swayed by the doubt of many, he stood on God's word that it was possible.

For security reasons, no American president ever carried a mobile phone. Barack still found a way around the impossible and became the first such president carrying in his pocket a new security tight version of the BlackBerry. Created for and named after him, the new secure phone took the name BarackBerry. It was all after he said it was possible that phone companies worked to invent a suitably security compliant presidential mobile phone. No earlier American president had ever overcome this huddle. The BarackBerry is probably one of the most expensive sought after mobile phones today, selling well above US$3000.   You can see the amount of power yielded by the tongue is greater than imagined. The scripture is explicit that there is power in words. *(Mat 12:37) For by your words you shall be justified, and by your words you shall be condemned.*

Truly by our words we shall be justified. It is not only through prayer that God hears us but even through mere discussions. Watch this: *Mal 3:16) Then those fearing Jehovah spoke together, each man to his neighbour. And Jehovah listened and heard. And a book of remembrance was written before Him for those who feared Jehovah, and for those esteeming His name.* These were people merely speaking to one another and not in a prayer meeting. It was neighbours speaking. It was what they spoke that attracted God to their conversation. God enjoyed the conversation as it showed that they feared God. These mere discussions caused God to call for a book of remembrance where these people were recorded for a reward. Can you see that our mere talking can really make or break us? What words do we say from time to time? What remembrance will our day to day words bring? God knows that we are pretty holy in church as we sing, preach and pray. What He now looks for is what we say in our ordinary day to day discussions because we spend more of our time, not at church, but in our ordinary environments. What are we saying when we are with others? Every word matters. Choose what to say. Remember that whatever you say, like the police say, may be used against you. What we say with our own mouths may be the difference between death and life. You have the right to remain silent until you know for sure what you intend to speak. Since it's a matter of life and death laid before us, we are tipped to choose life. *(Deu 30:19)... I have set before you life and death, blessing and cursing. Therefore, choose life, so that both you and your seed may live.* Clearly, we are to choose between death or life, blessing or cursing. To always remember that talking is choosing remains a virtue. Every time we speak we will be choosing between the things laid before us. Let's all choose life and blessing. Let's talk about what we choose. In all these things, remember that Israel (Jacob) is not cursed, knowing that whoever curses him will be cursed by God and whoever blesses him will likewise be blessed by the same God. Remember every time you utter a word, you are making a choice whose substance you will one day see in existence. God does not choose for us. We choose. Choose wisely from this day onwards and speak only what you want to see in existence. Your words are a powerful seed which takes no time to germinate and grow. Many times we just speak and leave it there without any thought of the result. The question is whether we really can leave it there. Never, it will germinate and become substance following us wherever we go. The devil works on permission. If you do not favour him with your confessions, then you have denied him a permit to operate in your life. Therefore do not issue him with that work permit but rather work to permit the power of The Lord to operate. It does not matter what you said or did in the past, once you change course and begin to speak the blood of Jesus Christ, believing and abiding in His word, all that was done in the past will be wiped away. The past will be counted as days of ignorance. *(Act 17:30) The times of ignorance therefore God overlooked.*

Learn to visualize the future and speak into it what things must be. Your children can become those you wish them to be if you speak your choices about them.

Greet them with a blessing. When you hold them as little babies, speak to them the greatness that shall follow them. Bless their mere existence and open lines of opportunity for them with mere words. Tell them as they giggle in your hands how they will lead a healthy life free of infections and all manner of body ailments. Speak wisdom and intelligence into their minds. They may seem too young to hear and understand but it's not about them but about you pronouncing what will become of them. It does not benefit the future of your offspring to always venge your anger about their irresponsible father or mother on them. I grew up hearing many mothers mock their children because of issues between the parents. I heard some telling the six months olds how they were as ugly as the father or how they would be poverty stricken like their father's family. This was being said in anger of perceived ill treatment by the father of these children. What the women forget is that it is them that will have the blessed opportunity to alter the course of these children as they are the first to hold them from birth and will in many cases stay with them for the first crucial years of their growing up. As a mother, how will you feel when you will see every negative word you pronounced on your child begin to come true in his or her growth? You will be quick to blame evil spirits, witches and the devil. Who bewitched your children? Nobody but you their mother who did not know the effect of spoken words. The fathers likewise put it all on their daughters, telling them they would be prostitutes like their mother, regardless of the mother being or not being one. While you spoke, little did you ever realize that you were choosing from what is before you? You forget that life is a vast domain full of unseen realities that can be called into existence by mere words. God said He has put before us life and death, blessing and cursing and it will not be up to Him anymore what must come our way. He says our choices will rule the day although He quickly hints that we must choose life so that we can live. Not only us, but also our children!

Can we blame God then? We can only blame the one responsible for shopping out of what is displayed. God has left that to us as individuals and parents. You are responsible for choosing for yourself and your offspring. The question is; what are you going to choose? In case you do not know how to make good choices, take wise advice from the Lord; *(Due 30:19)... Therefore, choose life, so that both you and your seed may live.* When my firstborn daughter Tino was born, I gave her a name and began to speak to her telling her she would be a great barrister, a powerful lawyer. I had wanted to be one myself and always admired the profession and yet opportunity had not come my way. I would tell her she would be everyone's lawyer of choice and that it was certainly going to come true. Growing up, she seemed here and there to face challenges with her high school work although generally she was intelligent. Changing schools would have cost her as our work took us from place to place. At her boarding school, her third high school, she had a few health challenges but that was the school to help her tackle her A levels whose examinations she passed very well. She was basing her efforts on a promise I would send her to a University abroad. Once she passed her exams, her part was done and I had to fulfil mine. This saw her reading law at Staffordshire University. She studied further at a Canadian law school and later answered a call to the bar. Today she is a recognized law practitioner right in the words of her father. The same has followed all my children wherever they go. They are blessed because I speak it to them not only in prayer but even when holding them as babies. I chose that for them.

Chapter Seventeen

You Deserve Better

Never ever concede to the wiles of the devil and feel that you are an outcast or that you do not deserve better in this life and that to come. You do not only deserve better but have it in Christ Jesus. It is laid upon your lips. Learn to speak of the great love of God which comes with His great provision. Certainly, joy will come your way. David knew this and he would wake up in the morning and choose to be happy. He woke up to confess the day into joy and happiness before he started it and all became like he declared. *(Ps 118:24) This is the day which the LORD hath made; we will rejoice and be glad in it.* He chose to rejoice. He chose to be glad in the day and it all worked to his confessions. In the same day, there were weeping and regrets for others depending on what they chose and declared in their own words. Speaking is choosing. Never forget that. Let your choices be clear. Speak life. Speak victory. Speak righteousness. Speak working for The Lord. Speak staying in the house of The Lord. Speak plenty. Speak good health and healing. Speak joy. Speak hope into your marriage. Speak a future into your children. Speak ministry. The Lord is faithful, all is laid before you.

Worry not about the words of mongers and gossipers. Be more concerned about your own confessions. You are more exposed to the power of your own confessions than the words of strangers. Remember to speak well of other Christians and leaders appointed and anointed by God regardless of their denominations. Believe the word of those appointed to speak into your life by The Lord, submitting yourself for correction and rebuke. Mind not that your error may leak or be gossiped around, rather mind disappointing Him who chose you. Respect more established believers, taking their advice seriously without exhibiting any pride. It is never wise to say that you don't mind what people say so long God loves you as you cannot fellowship sufficiently without others. Rather find out what separates you from other people and fix it if it's your own error, being wise that you do not become a servant of other people's believes and gossip. Do not underestimate God's calling on other people lest you be cursed in your own judgment. Remember to pray for the peace of Jerusalem for in doing so you bring peace to your church, home and personal life. Pay what you owe to those who once came to your rescue so that they may continue to speak well of you knowing their complaints are heard by The Lord as there is a cause. Learn to be slow to speak and quick to listen for such is what God instructs. Silence is golden when amidst those outspoken for vanity. In your entire goings in and out, bless Israel for he cannot be cursed. You are also under the same blessing with Israel as you are also a child of Abraham by faith in Christ. You are an empowered covenant person so you cannot be cursed. No plan or weapon designed against you can succeed. Any tongues speaking against you, accusing you, falsely bearing witness against you, or trying to judge or curse you, you shall have the authority to condemn. *(Isa 54:17) No weapon that is formed against you shall be prosper; and every tongue that shall rise against you in judgment, you shall condemn. This is the inheritance of the servants of Jehovah.* Forget not that words are things. Words are life, words are salvation, words are money, words are children, words are marriages, words are healing, words are peace, words are joy, and words are success, words are business, words are ministry and words are things. Words can also be those negative things depending on what is being confessed. Term your mouth by the transformation of your mind which comes by the hearing of the word of God. Make the right choices and speak them into existence in the name of The Lord Jesus Christ for all is laid before you. You are on your way to seeing the glory of The Lord in many ways and angles of your life, therefore be vigilant and give the enemy no room.

Speaking of choices, remember the major lesson about how the rightful heir was disinherited due to greed and lack of vision. Esau lost the unthinkable due to lame choices. He openly cried for red soup which was not by any shred of imagination comparable to the value of his birthright. He was fooled by the thought that birth rights were a naturally ascribed blessing and could not be exchanged by mere words. He thought words were simple noises and sound. They are not mere sound and noise; they are powerful and able to change the whole world. Through words all things were created. Through words God blessed Abram to become Abraham the father of nations. Through words Christ cleansed the ten lepers without touching any one of them. Through words we confess to our forgiveness and salvation. Through words two strangers agree to stay together as husband and wife and bear children. The two become bound closer than those born in the same house. Words are powerful. Mind the words you say and be aware each and every one of the words you say will one day meet with you as a blessing or a curse. Words cannot be washed away in the storm or flood. You will always grow to become a product of your own confessions. Do not be like Esau who lost it all through words. He exalted soup above his birthright and swore the heirship away describing it as something that he did not need and would rather have soup. The fear of hunger pushes people to do and say what they would otherwise not wish to. During the credit crunch, in the midst of which this book is written, it has been noticed that more and more people have bowed to many forms of pressure due to the high cost of living while the USA and Britain have led the worst job losses. There is need to watch what you say when hungry.

Esau later cried bitterly for his birthright. It was only at the point when his brother Jacob was blessed in his place that he realized how lethal his words had been. He wished he could turn everything around to get his birthright restored but it was too late. If said words could easily be unsaid, Esau could have done that at this desperate hour. His father had already blessed his young brother Jacob. Isaac his father literally told Esau there was nothing he could do for him as he had already blessed his brother. He plainly told Esau he had blessed Jacob making him lord over him and giving him his brothers for servants and workers. His father actually said he had sustained Jacob with provision. *(Gen 27:37) And Isaac answered and said to Esau, Behold! I have made him your lord, and all his brothers I have given him for servants. And with grain and wine I have supported him. And what shall I do now to you, my son?* All this was achieved by words only. On hearing this, Esau was devastated and he cried bitterly as he knew the power of those announcements would hold. He felt and became inferior from that day. There is nothing physical their father Isaac did. He just spoke some words concerning each of them and the boys began to become the products of their father's and their own utterances. Words are powerful.   Learn to expect good things to happen to you. Remember you deserve better than you think. Condition yourself to be pleasantly surprised, not always keeping your ears open in anticipation of bad news. Do not agree with your enemy that you will always be hearing and seeing the negative. Remember the love of God is not measured through physical blessings but His peace and victory in the inner person. Although you may have gone through so many hurtful situations in the recent past, learn to know that your God has good plans for you. Plans to prosper you and lift you out of the dirt. God cannot plan against you. He is on the drawing board planning good for those who fear His name. Never blame The Lord for hardships and sufferings for He does not design that for you. If you blame it on God, who then will be your deliverer? Believe Him; He has good plans for you. *(Jer 29:11) I alone know the plans I have for you, plans to bring you prosperity and not disaster, plans to bring about the future you hope for.*

Learn to think, believe and hope for better things for situations do not respond to prayer only but also to thoughts. God can read and fulfil your thoughts. *(Eph 3:20) Now to Him who is able to do exceeding abundantly above all that we ask or think...*This scripture is telling us that God can do according to what we think or ask. He can do greater than that. It helps to think good and positive. Living a life of faith and hope will keep doors open for the fresh air from above to blow through everything that involves you. Do not describe yourself using proverbs of lack, misery and hopelessness but gird yourself for the new things you believe The Lord will usher into your life. I listened to a BBC reporter who read the inscription in Morgan Tsvangirai's house on the news hour. For all what he had gone through, including detentions and battering, reporters may have expected a suicidal note in his house. They were enthused to read this one on the wall; *I do not pray for enemies to die but that they* *may live to see my success.* Imagine that coming from a politician. He believed in better things besides recent years of toil and surely he was one day inaugurated into being the second prime minister of independent Zimbabwe after Robert Mugabe who became president after the constitutional changes of 1990. Esau realized when it was too late that his utterances had come to roost. I urge you by the grace of our soon to come Lord Jesus Christ to be vigilant and guard jealously that which Christ Jesus has done in your life so that your children and their children will have something to testify concerning your walk with God. It was the work of Christ to liberate you; it's now your work to maintain that freedom. Jesus did for you what you could not do for yourself and it is now your turn to do what you can achieve through His spirit and grace. Guard your freedom against all forms of enslavement. Never give up. Jealously guard all things that The Lord has done for you. Nothing should ever come between you and your God. Allow no friend or material wealth to put you under siege. *(Gal 5:1) For freedom Christ has set us free; stand firm therefore, and do not submit again to a yoke of slavery.* You deserve better than the soup. Do not settle for it. You deserve the promises of Him who called us from darkness to light. You deserve the birthright that is in the new birth in Christ. You deserve the benefits of the new covenant which speaks of better things. You deserve eternal life where we shall live forever more in the presence of our God. We shall behold the beauty of The Lamb sitting at the right hand of The Father. You deserve to see the glory of The Lord.

Through the work of the cross, you deserve better than the soup. I say you deserve, not that I imply you earned it but because it has already been worked for, suffered for and died for by Him who loved us; Jesus Christ. You therefore could not just settle for anything when so much has been done to lift you higher. Once you have accepted Him, Jesus would like you to have it all. He would like to see you in good health both physically and spiritually. Jesus would know that He did not die in vain if He saw you happy and peaceful. You deserve better. *(3Jn 1:2)* *Beloved, I wish above all things that though mayest prosper and be in health, even as thy soul prospereth.*